Stepping Into Power

The Intuitive Path

Amanda Beth Johnson

© 2026 Amanda Beth Johnson

Published in the United States of America

All rights reserved worldwide

Authentic Endeavors Publishing/Spirit Book Endeavors

No part of this book may be reproduced by any mechanical, photographic, or electronic process, or in any form of audio or digital recording, nor may it be stored in any retrieval system, transmitted or otherwise, be copied for public or private use – other than for fair use as a brief quotation embodied in articles and reviews without prior written permission of the author, illustrators or publisher.

Authentic Endeavors Publishing
Scranton, PA 18505

Stepping Into Power

ISBN: 978-1-967041-90-9 (Paperback)
ISBN: 978-1-967041-91-6 (Ebook)
Library of Congress Control Number: 2026905285

Interior Design by Amit Dey

Table Of Contents

A Note on Language

Throughout this book, I use the word *Source* to describe the Divine, the higher power, the life force, the energy of love that flows through all that is. In my own training and practice, particularly in ThetaHealing®, I was taught to use the phrase "Creator of All That Is." For me, *Source* carries that same essence, but with a wider resonance.

You might call it God, Spirit, Universe, Creator, Great Mystery, or something else entirely. The words don't matter as much as the energy behind them. The language of the sacred is deeply personal.

As you read, I invite you to translate *Source* into the word or feeling that feels true for you. Whatever name you choose, it's all pointing toward the same infinite love and intelligence that connects us all.

Testimonials

I had the privilege of meeting Amanda Johnson over two years ago, and through a shared process of personal evolution, something deep and unexpected happened. I developed a profound love and respect for everything she carries within her. Amanda is one of those rare souls who is relentlessly committed to helping the people around her grow, heal, and rise. She turns the hardest parts of her own life into medicine, weaving her experience into healing for the world.

Anyone who has ever read her work knows instantly that she bleeds raw authenticity. She doesn't shy away from the shadows—she walks straight into them. And that's exactly where the real healing begins. That's where the light is most needed. And that's exactly the kind of lighthouse she is.

Amanda doesn't just talk about transformation; she embodies it. And anyone lucky enough to cross paths with her feels it.

J.D. Radewan, Transformational Shaman and Friend

I am incredibly grateful for Amanda Beth's healing work during the most difficult time of my life. After losing my child, I was overwhelmed by grief, and she has been a guiding light in my journey toward healing. Through a Chakra Scan and Energy Clearing, I felt an immediate release of tension and a deep sense of peace in my body. Her compassion and intuition have helped me process my grief in a gentle, transformative way. I feel more balanced, grounded, and hopeful with every session, and I can't thank her enough for the support and healing she's brought into my life.

Mary Brown, Texas

As a small business owner, I came into my session with Amanda Beth feeling like I was standing at a crossroads — overwhelmed, stuck, and weighed down by external energies that were hitting harder than usual.

Since our session, things have truly shifted. I've been transforming daily — staying in my energy, being mindful of my words, saying no when things don't align, and focusing on what I can actually control in the present. I'm showing up with more grace for myself and feeling more grounded and clearer in my day-to-day.

During the session, I felt a big energetic release. Since then, things have been settling in both subtle and powerful ways. I've felt more connected, more protected, and more at peace with where I am.

I'd absolutely recommend Amanda Beth. She makes the process feel safe, supportive, and aligned. Most importantly, she's deeply genuine — and that makes all the difference."

Sarah Gordon, Founder, Holistic Gypsiez

Dedication

This book is dedicated to those who helped shape my journey, whether through love, challenge, support, or simple presence. Many of you will never know how deeply you influenced my path, and I hold you with immense gratitude.

It is also dedicated to those who feel a stirring for something more. If you are searching for empowerment, meaning, or a deeper sense of purpose, may this book serve as a gentle guide and a reminder that you are not alone.

Acknowledgments

This book did not come into being alone.

I begin with gratitude for Source, the steady presence that guided this work long before I understood what it would become. Every insight, every moment of clarity, and every word offered here was shaped through connection, listening, and trust. I am deeply thankful for that guidance and for the wisdom that continues to unfold through it.

I am also grateful for the many teachers, mentors, coaches, and guides who supported me along the way, some through encouragement, some through challenge, and some simply by being present at the right moment. Not everyone who shaped this journey knows the role they played, and not every contribution was obvious at the time. Still, each one mattered.

To those who held space for my questions, my doubts, and my growth, thank you. To those who walked beside me quietly, offering steadiness rather than answers, your presence made a difference. I also acknowledge the experiences that stretched me, unsettled me, and asked more of me than I thought I could give. Not all lessons arrived gently, but each one contributed to the clarity and depth found in these pages.

I extend sincere appreciation to Teresa Velardi and Authentic Endeavors Publishing for their guidance, patience, and support in bringing this body of work to life. Their belief in this project and their commitment to meaningful storytelling helped shape these words into a finished offering.

Finally, I offer gratitude to every reader who chooses to spend time with this book. Your willingness to reflect, question, and remember gives this work its purpose. This book exists because of connection, and it continues because of you.

Introduction

There comes a moment when the life you've built starts to feel too small. Not because you've failed, but because you've outgrown it. That's what this book is about: those moments when your soul whispers, *"There's more,"* and you finally decide to listen.

When you step into your power, it's not about steamrolling others or proving your worth. It's about breaking off the last molded pieces that never truly belonged to you. The pieces shaped by expectation. By "shoulds." By the polite, acceptable version of you that learned how to survive.

You are not becoming "too much." You are becoming *exactly enough.*

This is the shift, from surviving within the lines to living between them. It's the transition from performing to *being*, from filtering yourself to letting the full frequency of who you are hum through your bones.

Power, in its truest form, isn't loud. It doesn't demand. It's quiet, grounded, and rooted in self-trust. It's the knowing that you no longer need permission to exist fully.

When you begin to live from that place, something beautiful happens: Life stops being about managing perception and starts being about *experiencing truth.*

You stop scanning the room for approval and start feeling for resonance. You realize you don't have to fight for space; you *are* the space.

In this book, I'll share what that process looked like for me. The messy, unfiltered, deeply human parts of healing, the ones that never make it to Instagram quotes. The moments of clarity that arrived in the middle of chaos. The tears, the laughter, the awkward conversations, the quiet breakthroughs that changed everything.

Stepping into your power doesn't mean becoming someone new. It means remembering who you were before the world told you who to be.

If you've ever felt like your light was "too bright," If you've ever learned to shrink so others could stay comfortable, If you've ever whispered your truth because shouting it felt dangerous, then this book is for you.

Each chapter is an invitation to reclaim the pieces you've hidden or handed away. To stop apologizing for your intuition, your softness, your strength. To live as the whole, radiant being you already are.

We'll talk about boundaries, discernment, and the messy middle ground of growth. We'll dive into what it means to live transparently, to honor the ethics of your gifts, and to step into service without self-sacrifice. You'll find stories, reflections, and moments of realness, not perfection.

And through it all, I hope you feel seen. Because this isn't just my story, it's a mirror for your own.

So take a breath.
Settle in.

You don't have to know every next step. Just bring your curiosity, your courage, and the part of you that's ready to come home.

This is where the journey begins. The moment you remember: You were never meant to fit the mold. You were born to break it.

With abundant blessings,

Amanda Beth

Part One:

Early Awakening

Chapter 1 — Before I Could Read, I Could Feel
Rediscovering the language of intuition through
handwriting, energy, and empathy.

Chapter 2 — A Psychic in the Bible Belt, Go Figure
Learning how intuition survives in a culture shaped by
faith, caution, and the unspoken rules of belonging.

Chapter 3 — "Woo" on Pause
Motherhood, creativity, and rediscovering your gifts
through the ordinary rhythms of life.

Chapter 4 — This Isn't My Life... and How I Changed It
The moment of awakening that breaks the mold and
begins the journey home to yourself.

Chapter 1

**Before I Could Read,
I Could Feel**

***When you touch one thing with deep awareness,
you touch everything.***
Thich Nhat Hanh

From the very beginning, I knew things. Not from books or lessons, long before I could even read.

When people say they can "read a room," I always laugh a little. For me, it was never optional; it was the background noise of existence. I could sense when my parents were tense, when the neighbor was sick, when a phone call was coming before it rang. As a child, it didn't feel mystical; it was simply how the world communicated. Energy spoke louder than words.

It's no secret that I'm a Gen X'er. Raised in a time before cell phones and Google, we learned how to *feel* what was going on around us, quickly. For me, it wasn't just about reading the room.

3

It was reading the people, the furniture, the walls, the house, the land... and even the echoes of those who had come before. It was never just a trauma response. It was a full-body knowing.

My parents divorced when I was three years old. My Mom returning to Iowa, where I would grow up. Then there was me: a sun-haired, dirt-loving tomboy who built roads in a tractor-tire sandbox and was happiest surrounded by toy dump trucks and dandelions. I was a product of the Midwest, where nature raised you, and your imagination was your best friend. Their joint custody afforded Summers and Christmas breaks in Northern Ohio.

Growing up Midwestern

Growing up, the Midwest wasn't something I consciously thought about. I was just living my life. My parents worked hard. My mom worked the night shift, and my step-dad came and went with the demands of his on-call work. That was simply how life was in those early years. We lived in a small town where neighbors were neighbors. People looked out for one another. I don't think our front door was ever locked.

Life was simple. We lived in a small cottage-style home on a quiet street that stretched only two blocks long. Our house sat back from the street with a long, narrow gravel drive that passed a sprawling, prickly juniper bush. That bush had the most beautiful fragrance and stayed green year-round. It grew tiny purple berries that were fun to collect, though I never had a use for them. The challenge was picking them without getting scratched.

The front yard was long, narrow, and grassy, framed by two trees that guided the eye back to our block-style home with its tall, pointed roof. It seemed to reach for the sky. The cottage was painted white beneath a wide, green-shingled roofline. Each small window had green trim painted on either side to mimic shutters. The sidewalk ran parallel to the street, then ran up along the gravel drive to the corner of the house before turning sharply to the front door.

Perfectly trimmed yew hedges lined the walk, and tall, slender evergreens stood proudly at each front corner. Near the door, a large hydrangea or snowball bush spilled outward. Brick sections from the old chimney bordered the concrete pad, doubling as planters. Pill bugs gathered there in abundance. A narrow passage between the snowball bush and the soft yew branches led to the garden, a small, hidden pathway that felt like a secret.

The garden mirrored the long, narrow driveway on the other side of the lot; stretched long and narrow. Alongside the garden, ran a treasured grapevine border. Those grapes were incredible. Sweet, juicy, and bursting when you pop them into your mouth. The skins were tough and flavorless, but the fruit inside was everything. You had to learn to spit out the seeds.

We grew tomatoes, turnips, green beans, radishes, corn, squash, and carrots. My mom canned much of it for the winter months. I remember eating slices of turnips sprinkled with salt, straight from the blade of my step-dad's pocketknife, standing right there in the garden. The salt made the crisp bitterness just right. That memory still holds the warmth of him and the earth beneath our feet.

The backyard was my refuge. It was fenced in and had a secret latch that made it feel like my own world. I spent countless hours there under the giant maple tree and watchful care of our Labrador, Snuffy. She was steady and loyal, a quiet guardian of our family.

My fifth birthday brought a swing set, joining my cedar playhouse and tractor tire sandbox. The playhouse arrived on a delivery truck from my father. The scent of cedar was rich and comforting, like my grandmother's linens. The bark-textured siding made it feel like a real log cabin. Large four-panel windows lined two sides and the back, letting in plenty of light. Faint orange spray paint marks from shipping remained inside, a small reminder that this little house had traveled a long way to reach me.

For that birthday, my mom made a clown piñata from scratch. She used a balloon and layers of newspaper, carefully glued together with a flour and water paste. The ears were oversized and floppy, shaped from grocery bags. All the neighborhood kids came. I wasn't in school yet, and it felt special to share my world with them. There were hamburgers, hot dogs, and all the familiar sides. I remember the sadness I felt when we finally broke the piñata open. It hurt to destroy something my mom had made with such care.

Our cottage was small, and the rooms flowed into one another. Arched doorways led to the galley kitchen and a short hallway. On one side stood a tall cupboard filled with towels, linens, and first-aid supplies. Across from it was a tiny bathroom with a shower stall, toilet, and a small hanging sink. There was barely room for a towel bar. The hallway opened into my parents' bedroom, where a closet with sliding doors took up most of one wall.

Upstairs was my space. One large loft stretched across the entire footprint of the house. The stairs creaked, announcing anyone who came up. The hardwood floors shone like glass. Small attic spaces lined the walls, and one became my crafting nook. I kept scissors, glue, and crayons there, inspired by the crafts I saw on our small, nine inch, black-and-white television. It sat awkwardly on a large end table in the living room, but it was ours.

I had a small table with bright red and blue poppy-like flowers against a dark blue background. Two perfectly sized chairs completed the set, framed in shiny chrome with white plastic seats. A raised plastic edging around the table top kept supplies from sliding off. I was never very good at cleaning up. Dried glue and bits of paper and glitter littered my crafting area.

The walls were painted bright green. My bed had heavy wooden head and footboards, covered with a golden yellow bedspread that reversed to a gingham pattern with tiny pink flowers. The open box springs made a comforting sound when I rocked myself to sleep.

My grandma lived farther away. Her home always smelled like comfort and love, wrapped in the scent of VO5 hair oil. She worked as a school cook and greeted us with open arms, calling out, "My babies, my babies." We stayed late when we visited, eating dinner and ice cream. She softened just for me, even though it annoyed my step-dad that I got special treatment. The Lawrence Welk Show always played before we left, I loved watching the bubbles float across the screen.

Her recipes live on through me. Sweet rolls, white bread, and her famous holiday soft and fluffy cut-out sugar cookies. She iced them lightly, added a few bright sprinkles, sometimes pink ones, her favorite color. To this day, my family carries on that tradition, decorating simply, with creamy white, buttercream frosting and just a pinch of sprinkles.

This was growing up in the Midwest. Simple pleasures. Manicured lawns. Gardens that fed both body and spirit. A deep respect for family, routine, and tradition.

I walked the few short blocks to school each day, wearing a simple white button-down cardigan on cool mornings. I wasn't allowed to knock on my friend's door on the way. Her family might be disturbed. That rule came from our home, since my mom slept during the day after working nights. Her mom often sent her out with peeled orange segments in a clear baggie. She always shared. It was cool, juicy, and bright, already prepared with care. I remember pacing the sidewalk, softly singing her name while I waited, never daring to knock.

Living the Other Life

Summers with my father in Ohio were different. That version of life was neat and proper, buttoned up in a way my everyday world was not. There were rules. Expectations. A clear sense of how things should look and how people should behave. It was a sharp contrast to my free-spirited nature and my stepmother's structured world.

My stepmother was ten years older than my mother and had lived a more affluent, child free life before meeting my father. I was about five when I came into her world. She was prim and proper, a woman who had mastered etiquette and presentation. Red nail polish was forbidden. I was told I could not paint my nails at all unless they were long enough to be worthy of polish. Red remains my favorite color to this day, a quiet rebellion.

Much of the strictness centered around etiquette and appearance. How one sat. How one ate. Which fork to use. Where the napkin belonged.

She had clear rules about clothing. No T shirts with writing or graphics. Belts were always worn if there were belt loops. Shirts were always tucked in. White shoes, purses, or belts were never worn before Memorial Day and absolutely never after Labor Day. Laundry followed a precise weekly rotation. When I started a new school in seventh grade, she coordinated my entire wardrobe in red, white, and blue so every piece was interchangeable. I did love those red painter style pants.

She had not been able to have children in her previous marriage, so I was the first child she encountered in her adult life. I often accompanied her to ladies luncheons and formal outings, usually the only child present. While she was not unkind, I lived in an adult world, expected to observe and behave rather than play.

Still, I cherished the time with my father and stepmother. As their only child during those visits, I had all the attention during Christmas breaks and summer vacations. Her routines were steady and predictable, and because my visits were short, there were few chores or responsibilities placed on me. To me, it felt like a holiday, structured but light. When we were apart, her letters carried that same sense of order and care, reminding me that even for a brief time, I had been held at the center of her world.

My Box of Stationery

One of the few bridges between my stepmother and me came through handwritten letters. It began with a gift she gave me: a box of fine stationery. Cream colored, linen-textured trifold paper, printed in raised shiny black ink, my name and return address gracing the upper closure flap. The design was trimmed with bright green grass and dotted with red ladybugs. I was enchanted. Each letter I sent was sealed with a shining ladybug sticker, my version of a wax seal, official and proud. Small details that made the act of writing feel important.

The box itself felt special before I ever opened it. It was a rigid cardboard box covered in glossy cream-colored paper, the lid marked with a golden embossed oval. When I lifted it, the scent of ink and fresh paper rose up, and the note cards rested beneath a thick sheet of tissue, as if they were being protected. Opening that box always felt like opening a gift from her.

When I wrote to her, she wrote back. That simple exchange became our quiet ritual, our shared language. As I traced her cursive with my eyes, I could feel her presence lingering in the paper itself, carried through ink and intention. Even before I understood the words, I understood the feeling.

Opening that box was one of my earliest experiences of journaling, of reaching beyond the walls I lived within. Not because anything was wrong inside those walls, but because something in me longed for connection, for the feeling of being seen. Even during short visits, just a week or two at a time, I was the center of attention. That little box of stationery became a tether to those days, a quiet talisman connecting me to a version of myself that felt lighter, more alive.

At the time, I could barely write my own name. But sending a letter meant I would receive one in return, and that was the real magic. My stepmother always wrote in cursive, her script winding across the page. I don't remember who read the letters to me or how I understood what was written. I only remember how they felt. Before opening the envelope, I already knew the message inside. Her handwriting carried her energy, warm and structured, often affectionate, and it wrapped around me like a hug.

Looking back now, I see it clearly. Those pieces of paper were never just stationery. They were my first experience of connection through energy, of being heard, of being held in words. They taught me that something sent out into the world could be received with care.

Even now, I'm drawn to writing on index cards, roughly the same size as those trifold note cards from my childhood. I recognize how deeply they shaped my love for small, intentional spaces of expression. Years later, when we designed our wedding invitations, I was instinctively drawn to that same folded format. At the time, I didn't know why it mattered. I only knew it felt right.

Even then, I could sense that what flowed through me wasn't mine alone. It felt ancient and familiar, like the low hum I heard in the wind moving across the Iowa cornfields. The land itself carried memory and story, and somehow, so did I.

The Energetics of Ink

It wasn't just her letters. I could feel *anyone's* handwriting. Everyone wrote in cursive, which left the most profound energetic imprint. Early on, I didn't know how to read the words, but I could feel the frequency they carried. Happiness, anxiety, love, disappointment, it was all there, woven into the ink like a coded vibration. Even once I learned to read, the written words had far less meaning than the feelings I would receive, just looking at the paper. Handwriting wasn't just symbols; it was energy.

For Harry Potter fans, it was like every note became a howler, though not always in a negative way. The emotions would jump off the page. Some were intense. Some were subtle. But they all spoke. The paper held more than words; it held *presence*.

At the time, I assumed everyone experienced this. Ironically, most people only notice if something's written in all capital letters or sharply slanted in a moment of rage. That's basic graphology. But, what I experienced went far beyond the visible. It was a psychic imprint, a soul-level transmission through pen and paper. I hear and feel the tones of the intention behind the mere words on the paper.

From the earliest days, I could feel the emotions and intentions behind written words, long before I could actually read them. A letter didn't just carry information; it brought the *essence* of the person who wrote it.

As I learned to read, I noticed something that fascinated me: the words on the page didn't always match the energy they emitted. A note might say something polite, even kind, but the handwriting carried frustration, sorrow, or hesitation. Or it could be the opposite, the words were brief and formal, but the ink practically vibrated with warmth and excitement.

I remember tracing my finger along the edges of letters in picture books, and each word had a texture. "Love" felt warm and pink. "Sad" was a deep, heavy blue. "Tomorrow" shimmered like sunlight on water.

At first glance, it might sound like synesthesia, a neurological trait where one sense automatically activates another. Some people see letters or numbers in specific colors, taste words, or experience sound as shape or color. For those who have it, these sensations are consistent and involuntary, the same letter always the same color, the same sound always the same feeling. It is a real and well-documented blending of the senses, and it is far more common than most people realize.

But this wasn't that.

What I was experiencing was not a crossing of senses so much as a crossing of feeling energy and its meaning. It was empathy meeting language. The words did not just look like something. They felt like something. They carried emotion, tone, and resonance. I wasn't perceiving color or texture for its own sake. I was sensing the emotional weight of the energy held inside the ink itself.

This is an important distinction, because many people experience this kind of emotional sensing without ever labeling it. They feel the mood in a room before a word is spoken. They sense tension, warmth, sadness, or joy without knowing why. They respond to language not just intellectually, but emotionally and physically. That, too, is a form of perception. It is far more common, and far more human, than we are often taught to believe.

That sensitivity became both my compass and my curse. I'd read birthday cards or handwritten notes and feel the genuine emotion behind the ink. Sometimes the words said, "I'm fine," but the energy whispered, "I'm falling apart."

I thought that was normal. I thought handwriting was just another way of hearing people's hearts. It wasn't until later that I learned most people only saw the words and understood them in the limits of a dictionary meaning.

Later, in my formal study of graphology, I learned the "rules" for analyzing handwriting, including slants, pressure, letter formation, and spacing. But what I could sense went far beyond that. For me, handwriting functioned like a psychic key, much as Tarot cards or runes do for other intuitives. It was a doorway. Once I saw the script, it was almost as if the writer was standing right in front of me.

I could feel them. Their mood. Their intention. Sometimes, even the circumstances around them when they wrote it. And here's the thing, they didn't need to be anywhere near me. Not the same building, not the same state. I could read the energy from a distance, carried in the ink and paper.

The paper never seems to lose that emotional impact. One of my favorites is to "read" what people write in the front of their books. The passion that is present when a book has been gifted versus the firm commitment of a name when it is marked for sheer ownership. But even then, there is the energy of pride in owning a book to share rather than a name written because the book was issued to the writer.

I once had a supervisor who loved to give books as gifts. She would open the cover, write a personal message, and then sign the author's name, as if she herself had written the book. She thought it was charming, a playful way to make the gift feel more intimate. It wasn't until she learned that a local author was a family member of mine that her tone shifted. She suddenly felt embarrassed. In that moment, she realized she hadn't just personalized a book. She had impersonated an author. She had borrowed the authority and identity of someone who had done something she herself had never imagined doing.

That moment stayed with me, because it revealed something subtle and powerful about publishing. There is an energetic shift that happens when you put your words into the world. Authorship carries weight, whether we acknowledge it consciously or not. I was once told there are only three paths that make someone "famous" in this very particular way. You can be an actor, an athlete, or an author. Each of these roles requires visibility. Each requires stepping forward and allowing yourself to be seen. And each involves accomplishing something that most people quietly believe they could never do themselves.

Publishing a book places you in that space. Not because of ego or attention, but because you have chosen to make your voice visible. You have taken something internal and made it tangible. Ink holds energy. Words carry intention. When you commit them to paper, you are no longer hiding behind ideas or drafts or potential. You are saying, this is mine. This is what I know. This is what I am willing to share.

I never imagined myself here. In college, I felt lucky just to finish a paper and turn it in on time. Publishing my own work was never a goal, never a plan, never something I believed was meant for me. Yet here I am. Writing this, my second book. Claiming my voice. Allowing myself to be seen.

This is the energetics of ink. The courage it takes to make yourself visible. The power that comes from choosing not to hide. The quiet transformation that happens when you step into authorship, not just of a book, but of your own story.

You do not have to be loud to be powerful. Sometimes courage is simply allowing yourself to be visible.

Feeling First, Logic Later

School was confusing for someone like me. Everyone wanted facts and formulas. I wanted feelings and flow. When teachers said, "Show your work," my inner voice screamed, "But I *felt* the answer!"

Being dyslexic and dysgraphic added another layer. The world wanted linear. My brain gave them spirals. Still, I adapted. I built bridges between the felt sense and the logical one, learning how to translate the unseen into something others could understand. That's probably when my future healer self began to form, the interpreter between two worlds.

I didn't yet have the language for "energy work," but I already understood it on a cellular level. I knew when someone's energy was closed. I could sense when a friend's sadness wasn't really about what they were saying. Sometimes I'd blurt out truths that made adults uncomfortable. I wasn't trying to be rude; I just didn't know how *not to know.*

When the Words and the Energy Don't Match

One of my favorite things has always been reading old journals, letters, and handwritten texts, not for the story alone, but for the *energy* that seeps between the lines. I've often noticed that the most valid message isn't always in the words, but in the way the hand moves the energy across the page.

Once, a friend of mine, an author who wrote for Harlequin Romance, received a handwritten fan letter on lined notebook paper. It was four or five pages long, the writer's attempt to describe who they thought the author was, based entirely on reading all her novels. Their interpretation of her personality and life was remarkably detailed, and, knowing her as I did, not entirely wrong.

She was so taken aback by the letter that she asked me to look at the handwriting.

What I picked up went beyond content: I could feel the eagerness and almost giddy anticipation this fan felt as they began writing. But I could also see the exact points in the letter where they hesitated, pulled back, and censored themselves. There were moments where their energy faltered, as though unsure if they'd gone too far or revealed too much.

I relayed everything I felt to her, down to the subtle pauses and shifts in tone. She found my reading both fascinating and affirming. In the end, she typed back, a simple, polite response, identifying their character as reflected in their handwriting, and that was the last she ever heard from them.

How the Information Flows

Over time, I've realized that this way of reading handwriting from others isn't about memory, it's about channeling. The information comes through me, flows to the person who needs it, and then leaves. I don't always retain the details, because they're not mine to keep. My role is to be the bridge or messenger between Source and others.

Even today, although I no longer actively use handwriting analysis in my professional work, the way I first learned to *sense* energy remains at the root of everything I do. It was my first real knowing that I could connect with someone's energy without being in the same room, or even the same part of the world.

There are times I have been reported as providing brilliant information. I am often shocked myself that eloquent and timely wisdom spews from me. It is purely channeling, as I didn't have that level of specificity in my repertoire.

I used to squawk at the term "channeling." It felt too woo-woo. However, by definition, that is what happens when you can quiet the chatter and tune in. When I approach specific tasks, I start by quieting my mind and calling in Source and my Guides to assist me in my highest and best good. Much of the time, when I am in the flow, the information is just there, without me having to request it.

The Untrained Empath

Like so many sensitives, I didn't understand what was happening at first. Honestly, it could be overwhelming. I had no filter, no shield, no permission-based practice. I simply *received* all the time.

As many empathic children, I began to shut some of it down.

In my family, intuition was quietly accepted but never formally taught. My relatives didn't scoff when I said I "just knew" something, but they also didn't lean in with fascination. It was like knowing how to breathe: a thing you did, not a thing you discussed.

The gift was there, passed down quietly through generations, wrapped in practicality. We didn't perform rituals or light candles. We gardened, cooked, prayed, and listened to what the wind or the heart had to say.

That's what happens when the world doesn't teach you how to hold your gifts. The input becomes too much. Without boundaries, without containment, intuition can turn into exhaustion. So we silence it, suppress it, or deny it altogether.

But the truth of our abilities never leaves us. It waits.

Creating My Own Ethical Code

When I finally realized that not everyone experiences intuition the way I do, I also realized how much responsibility comes with this gift. Just because I *can* sense something doesn't mean I *should* say it. That pause, that moment of discernment, became my first lesson in what I now think of as my personal code of ethics.

For me, intuition has never been about performance. I'm not here to shock people with what I know. I'm here to serve, to translate, to support healing and growth along their journey. That requires discernment: what to share, what to hold, and when to simply stay quiet.

Early on, I learned that reading energy without permission felt invasive, almost like eavesdropping on a private conversation. The information might come to me, but that didn't make it mine to pass along. That understanding shapes the way I approach every client session now. Consent isn't a formality, it's sacred. It's the doorway that allows trust to flow, and without it, there is no healing.

There was a time I shared something I sensed without realizing it wasn't already common knowledge. The words slipped out naturally, because the information felt so ordinary to me, like I had just overheard it somewhere publicly. But the look on the other person's face stopped me cold. They hadn't told me that detail. There was no way I could've known.

In that moment, I realized I had crossed a line I hadn't even seen. What I thought was small talk had actually been an unfiltered piece of intuitive information. I hadn't paused to ask myself, *Did I learn this through human channels, or did this come straight through my intuition?* That pause matters.

It was an uncomfortable lesson, but one that shaped how I handle conversations today. Now, if I receive information intuitively, I don't automatically share it. Instead, I'll gently test the waters with neutral questions, feeling out whether it's appropriate to continue. It's a softer, more respectful approach that honors both the sacredness of the information and the person receiving it.

Over time, as I became more aware of what I was perceiving, I developed a personal set of rules. A quiet code of ethics around reading energy, from the handwriting I felt to the intuition I trusted. No one taught me this. It came from within, rooted in reverence.

Rule #1: Not all energy is mine to read.
If someone hasn't permitted me, I wouldn't intentionally open myself to the deeper frequency of their energy or writing. Just as

you wouldn't eavesdrop on a whispered prayer, I knew intuitively that I had to honor the boundary of the page.

Rule #2: Discernment matters.

There's a difference between reading for content and reading for *intention*. I could feel the earnestness, the emotional truth of a message, but I also learned that not everything needs to be understood psychically. Sometimes the words are enough.

Rule #3: Protect your container.

I didn't have the words back then, but I knew the feeling. If I took in too much emotion, energy, or sorrow, I'd get sick. I had to learn when to tune in, when to close down, and when to *simply observe*.

"Having the Words"

I want to pause here and say something about this. There's no doubt that I receive information from many sources. Over time, I've learned to process it in my own way and to create a method that helps others with my gifts. But when I was first learning my way through all of this, I felt utterly lost.

It's kind of like discovering that every practitioner has their own glossary. The same concept might be called three different things depending on who you ask. At first, I thought I was missing something important, like I wasn't smart enough to keep up. What I've learned is this: *don't get caught up in the words. What matters is not what it's called, but how you use it.* Growth comes from practice, presence, and honing your skills, not from memorizing the right vocabulary or symbols.

Information from intuition or Source does not usually arrive in words, but in impressions, images, or objects that carry meaning. These symbols are not fixed or universal. They are interpreted within the context of the person, the moment, and the question being explored. I'll explain this more fully later in this book.

The Foundation of Everything

Looking back, I see that those early years of feeling the written word laid the foundation for everything I do now. I may not read handwriting in my current work, but I still read energy. I still feel the imprint behind what's said or left unsaid.

Those same ethical principles apply. As a healer, I believe we're only meant to receive what a person is ready for. Even when Source offers information, we must *discern* what is appropriate, useful, and kind.

That's why I never call what I do mine solely. It's a *partnership* with the person, with Source, and with the energetic truth of the moment.

But that's a chapter for another day.

Closing Reflection

Our first awareness of intuition often comes before we even have words for it. For me, it was handwriting, feeling energy infused in ink before I could read a single sentence. We all have these subtle gifts, but as we grow, many of us are taught to dismiss them as imagination or coincidence. Yet intuition is our natural language, waiting for us to remember.

Journal Prompt

Reflect on your earliest memories of "just knowing" something or sensing energy. What was happening? How did it feel in your body? Did anyone encourage or dismiss that awareness? Write about how that memory shaped your relationship with your intuition.

____

____

____

____

____

____

____

____

Chapter 2

A Psychic in the
Bible Belt, Go Figure

Energy flows where attention goes.
Michael Beckwith

The Midwest is a land of good hearts and cautious souls. It's where faith and fear sometimes sit in the same church pew.

People pray for miracles, but they want them to look tidy, something that can be explained without shaking too many foundations.

I remember sitting through countless sermons where the pastor spoke of prophets and visions, but if you mentioned hearing your grandmother's voice in a dream, folks would tighten their smiles.

There was a constant, quiet rule: miracles happened in the Bible, not in Davis County.

As a child, I absorbed that double message: Yes, God was everywhere, but He preferred to act through approved channels.

That paradox soaked into me like rain into good soil, leaving me both rooted and restless.

As life moved forward, I began learning how to *temper* my connections more effectively. What I would later call intuition started as a quiet, internal pulse, a strange awareness that didn't seem to belong to my five senses but was just as real.

It was like a spiritual wiring harness built into my being. I didn't always use it, but it was always there, waiting. Ready to light up when I needed a little boost or a more profound knowing. It was that persistent nudge that led me to learn to call specifically for guidance.

As I honed this gift, I began to realize not everyone could *tune in* the same way.

That still baffles me. It's hard to explain what feels so natural to you, especially when no one ever talked about it growing up. I just *knew things.* Things I hadn't been taught. Things I couldn't have read in a book or picked up from someone else. While my family didn't "talk about" intuition, I was never hushed for knowing these things.

Growing up in the Midwest means you learn early what fits and what doesn't. Cornfields, casseroles, and the weather, those are safe topics. Energy work, intuition, and spirit communication? Those are "maybe keep that to yourself" topics.

Growing up intuitive in the Bible Belt is like carrying a secret you're not supposed to have. On Sundays, I'd sit in church hearing about heaven, hell, and sin, yet during the week, I was feeling things no one talked about. I'd know when someone was sick before they told me. I'd sense when a family fight was brewing before a word was spoken. To me, it wasn't spooky or wrong. It was just *true*.

But in the Bible Belt, truth comes with a rule. The rule was simple: if you "knew things you shouldn't" you were either crazy, lying, or worse, dabbling in "the devil's work."

I can't tell you how many times I swallowed back an intuitive knowing, afraid of the looks or whispers if I spoke it aloud. I was lucky in some ways. In my own family, psychic abilities weren't treated as strange or shameful, but they weren't necessarily taught or deliberately developed either. It was more of a quiet acknowledgment, something that existed without being made into a big deal. I was never scorned for knowing things, but I also wasn't given a roadmap for how to use these gifts.

It wasn't a mystical secret or a family scandal, it was just something that existed quietly, like an old quilt folded at the end of the bed. We all knew it was there; we just didn't talk about it much.

That's what many of us did: we shut it down. We played small. We tried to blend in. We laughed at the jokes about "crazy psychics" even when we *were* one. We did what we had to do to be safe.

In the early days, the word *psychic* didn't feel mystical or empowering. It felt dangerous. It was often tangled with assumptions of being unstable, delusional, or worse. To some, it meant psychotic. To others, it carried the weight of religious fear, whispered warnings about witchcraft or doing the devil's work. None of it was about who we actually were. It was about judgment, about falling outside the lines of what was acceptable, and learning very quickly that visibility came with consequences.

We nodded along in Sunday school even when we knew things the teacher couldn't explain. I have one friend who, at the ripe old age of 9, told the Sunday School teacher she was wrong. Needless to say, she was not welcomed back. Luckily, her mother was intuitive like her and never forced her to deny her knowledge.

The gift never really goes away. It just waits. Like a pilot light inside you, flickering quietly until you're ready to let it blaze again. For me, the reawakening came later, after loss, after upheaval, after realizing the life I was living wasn't mine. That's when I stopped caring so much about the whispers from others. That's when I realized: my knowing isn't a curse. It's my compass.

Being psychic in the Bible Belt taught me this: you don't have to defend your gift to anyone. You don't have to convince your skeptical uncle, or win over your pastor, or prove yourself to the neighbor who whispers behind your back. You only have to trust yourself and Source. The more you lean into that trust; the less fear of judgment has any power over you.

The question to ask yourself is, "Have you ever nurtured it?"

I've come to believe this is the ancient knowing we each carry into this life as souls. We are souls having a human experience. Some of us are older souls, with more threads woven into our tapestry. Others may be just beginning to learn how to trust that inner compass. But here's the truth: *we all have intuition.*

For some lucky ones, it's been nurtured since childhood. For others, it's been silenced, dismissed, mocked, or even punished.

I want to pause here and speak directly to those of you who shut down your gifts to fit in, to stay safe, or to avoid being "too much." Maybe you were told you were crazy, or dramatic, or wrong. Perhaps you were told to "stop making things up." Maybe, over time, you learned it was easier to lock that part of yourself away.

If that's you, I want you to know this: your intuition never left you. It has been patiently waiting. Waiting for the day you'd no longer give a damn about what anyone else thinks. Waiting for the day you'd feel the hunger to reclaim yourself.

That hunger, the thirst you feel right now as you read this, is your ancient knowing calling you home. It's your soul whispering: *Wake up. Remember. You were never broken. You were always whole. You just forgot for a while.*

Here's the gift: the moment you stop apologizing for your intuition, your gifts expand. The moment you choose to reawaken, the doors fly open. You don't need permission. You don't need validation. You only need to listen.

Imaginary Friends and Real Gifts

When I became a mother, I knew I wanted to parent differently. My daughter had imaginary friends, and I never once dismissed them. Who was I to say they weren't real? She wasn't afraid. She wasn't causing harm. She was simply in touch with something beyond the visible. I couldn't remember having imaginary friends myself, but I'm sure they would not have been discouraged if I did.

That became the foundation of how I parented: softer, gentler, with room for grace. I stepped back often to ask, "Does this really matter at the end of the day? Will this create a problem in her development, or is it simply her way of exploring who she is?"

Because I owned my own business, she was with me rather than in daycare. That gave me the luxury of letting her follow what interested her, to become her own sovereign person.

It wasn't always easy. She has a strong personality, just like her mother. But the freedom to make choices and experience opportunities at a young age allowed her to grow into a respectful, hardworking young woman who can discern for herself which friends, paths, and values are hers, and which are not.

Of course, she still had to navigate public school expectations. There, the rules were different than those at home. But at home, she always knew she had the grace and support to express herself, to test out her gifts, and to grow into who she really is.

As she moved into her teenage years, her intuitive gifts faded somewhat into the background, just as mine once did. I trust that in time she can return to them with the same deliberation and strength I eventually did.

Unlearning Fear

That's what I mean when I say that how you're raised, and how open your circle is shapes your relationship with intuitive gifts. Some families foster that connection, others fear it. For many of us, our journey begins not with encouragement, but with *unlearning the fear* we inherited.

Imagine what it would be like to grow up in a family where your gifts were not just tolerated, but actually taught, where someone sat you down and showed you how to use your intuition in purposeful, meaningful ways, like a "boarding school for Wizards" but at home.

I didn't have that, and maybe you didn't either. *Most of us didn't.* At best, some of us were given quiet acceptance. At worst, we were ridiculed or shamed into shutting down completely.

So when we begin to reawaken, that fear comes rushing back. It whispers: *What will people think of me? Will I lose my friends? Will I lose my community? Will I be labeled crazy, weird, or worse?*

Fear keeps us small. It convinces us that hiding is safer than being seen. But here's the truth: awakening constantly changes your circle. Just as friendships shift when you stop attending certain events or stop belonging to specific groups, they shift again when you choose authenticity over conformity... and sometimes over comfort.

The turning point comes when your desire to grow becomes greater than your fear of judgment. When you no longer concern yourself with what they will say because you finally know who you are. When the need to expand outweighs the risk of losing approval, *that* is when you can drop the fear that has held you hostage for so long.

Here's the miracle: once you put fear down, you discover you were never alone. There are coaches, guides, and healers who have walked this path before you, ready to help you step into your next level. You begin to attract others who are also awakening, creating a new circle that resonates with your soul instead of restraining it.

Unlearning fear is not about becoming fearless. It's about listening to your heart, your intuition, your soul, and your authenticity louder than you listen to the noise of other people's opinions. It's about choosing your own truth over their expectations.

That's when you step into your power; not the power to dominate or impress others, but the power to live as who you truly are. The freedom to expand, evolve, and embody your gifts without apology.

Dreams, Premonitions, and a Deeper Knowing

In my late teens, things began to intensify. I started *knowing* how social situations would unfold. I'd know who was going to show up, or what kind of energy the night would hold. I often brushed it off as a fluke, wishful thinking, or maybe just my anxiety trying to keep me safe.

However, hindsight has shown me that I wasn't imagining things. I was perceiving what hadn't yet arrived.

My dreams became especially vivid. One, in particular, haunted me from the age of 12 to 27. In it, I was the driver of a large white car that was struck hard by something significant, like a train. I died every time. The dream stopped suddenly when I was 27, the same year my husband died in a car accident, in a large white car. There was no train involved, but the damage to the vehicle was identical to the one in my dreams.

I still don't have the words to explain that. But I know what it taught me: our dreams are messengers. Sometimes from our Soul. Sometimes from Source. Sometimes, from our future selves, we try to get a message through the veil.

How could I have done anything differently with that dream premonition? Never owning a white car? I do know that life is precious and far too short. Hold your loved one deeply and say the words that matter.

A First Responder… With Second Sight

I became an Emergency Medical Technician (EMT) at just 18. Strange as it may sound, many of my dreams continued, and they became *predictive*. I would dream of accidents before they happened. I'd see the number of victims, the vehicles involved, even the types of injuries.

At first, I'd wake in panic, heart racing, as if I'd just lived through the crash myself. But over time, I learned to become the observer, not the participant. These dreams weren't for me to feel; they were information to help me *prepare.*

This pattern didn't stop with dreams. Sometimes I'd feel someone's physical pain before they ever showed up. My mother, a paramedic-turned-doctor, has the same gift. She feels discomfort in her own body, and sure enough, a patient arrives with the same complaint.

It's a strange gift, isn't it? Feeling something in your own body and asking: *Is this mine, or is it someone else's?* This is the epitome of being an empath.

I know of many who specialize in this modality, often called Medical Intuitives. They are all about the physical body, down to the intricate parts that make up each cell of the body. Frequently, their gifts presented without any formal "medical" training. They are an absolute godsend when modern medicine fails.

Ordained by Intuition (and the Internet)

After college, I transitioned from the intensity of emergency response to the world of support work, volunteering with the American Red Cross and working with children and families in crisis.

I still received information intuitively. It would often come through in unexpected ways: flashes, sensations, or just a knowing that couldn't be explained. Information flowed; I rarely fact-checked, it wasn't a thing yet.

The information I unconsciously attended to was of the most minor things; grabbing an extra snack for the car, only to find myself working late and missing a meal.

One day, I was so fortunate that a sweater had fallen out of the basket of clean clothes and had been left behind in the car. A child I held had gotten sick. My first impulse was to find a store, then I got that nudge to check the back seat.

A name would pop into my mind seconds before my phone rang. Occasionally, I'd "hear" a quiet inner nudge, *ask about her mother,* and it would open the exact doorway needed to move forward.

When I returned to Iowa, I reconnected with family, especially my aunt, who adored the Tarot. While that wasn't my preferred tool, we found ourselves drawn to the psychic shows traveling through the Bible Belt. Yes, that's as wild as it sounds: spiritual pop-ups in some of the most conservative corners of the country.

At the time, I was already making colorful teddy bears for juried craft shows. My aunt and I created colorful, cosmic, astrology-inspired dream pillows, chakra sets, and other metaphysical goodies, filled with herbs, intention, care, and ritual. Everything we offered was handmade, heart-infused, and energetically aligned.

Then came the readings. My aunt was an incredible clairvoyant, gifted in Tarot.

I remembered all those times I had received powerful insight just from someone's handwriting. I had already earned a degree in psychology and brushed up on graphology, the formal analysis of handwriting. So I started offering readings as a *Psychographologist,* blending my degree in psychology and my intuitive perception.

But there was a catch.

To legally offer psychic readings at these events, especially in the Bible Belt states like Kansas, Kentucky, Missouri, Oklahoma, or Ohio, you had to be an *ordained minister.* Apparently, it wasn't "soothsaying" if it was framed as a *Spiritual gift* under a religious umbrella.

A spiritual gift is often defined as a special ability or talent given by the Holy Spirit to a Christian to serve God and build up the Christian community (the Church). These are supernatural endowments, not natural talents, distributed by God for the good of the body of believers, such as prophecy, healing, teaching, or administration. The purpose of spiritual gifts is to promote unity, encourage others, and fulfill God's mission in the world.

I went online, downloaded the forms, wrote out a check, and mailed it off. A few weeks later, I had my official ordination wallet card and certification. My aunt and I agreed we would only use it to "practice our gifts of the Spirit."

Soon after, we participated in a formal ordination ceremony in Wichita, Kansas, led by the Infinite Source Church. It was nondenominational, reverent, and profoundly moving. I remember sitting on a stage surrounded by others, stepping into their path as Spiritual practitioners.

I remember filing into the chairs for the ceremony, just following the group. While seated, listening attentively, a calm fell over the entire room. Then a warmth with only a twinge of goose bumps.

It felt sacred. It felt like *Truth*. It felt as if the whole world had stopped.

Not the take-your-breath-away kind of stop, but as if the momentum of the Earth itself had stilled. Just for a heartbeat, long enough to feel the frequency change, the air thickens with knowing, the veil between what is and what could be split open.

It wasn't fear. It wasn't pain. It was a pause, pure and deliberate, as though the universe held its breath, waiting for me to catch mine.

In that suspended stillness, there was only awareness. Only truth. And for that one impossible moment, I knew everything was exactly as it should be.

Why Someone Seeks a Reading

People seek readings for many reasons, but rarely because they want to be told what to do. A reading is not about handing your power to someone else. It is about gaining perspective. When you are inside your own life, it can be difficult to see clearly. Patterns feel personal. Emotions blur the edges. A reading offers a wider view, helping you understand what is influencing you beneath the surface and where your energy is asking for attention.

Some people seek a reading during times of transition, grief, or uncertainty. Others come when they feel stuck, disconnected, or out of alignment with themselves. A reading can help name what you already sense but haven't been able to articulate. It can confirm intuition, highlight blind spots, or simply bring clarity to a moment that feels confusing or overwhelming.

An ethical reading does not predict your future or remove your choice. It supports your awareness. It helps you understand where you are, what energies are at play, and what options may be available to you. Ultimately, the purpose of a reading is not answers, but understanding. Not direction, but discernment.

When Not to Seek a Reading

There are also times when a reading may not be supportive. If you are feeling emotionally dysregulated, desperate for answers, or looking for someone to make decisions for you, it may be worth pausing. A reading is not meant to replace medical care, mental health support, or personal responsibility. It is also not meant to soothe anxiety by predicting outcomes or offering certainty where none exists. When fear is driving the question, the information received can feel overwhelming or misused. In those moments, grounding, support, and stabilization often come first. A reading can wait.

Navigating Ethics in a Sea of Energy

In my early days of psychic readings and shows, everyone claimed to be a reader. Healers were not in the circles or familiar to me.

With the progress and availability of the internet, everyone is offering classes and certifications in all sorts of psychic and healing practices. I have been a fellow student and mentored by others. I have encountered extraordinary practitioners who have no formal training or certification. The opposite is also true; I have come across certified practitioners who don't measure up.

Even now, with several certifications in ThetaHealing®, homeopathy, shamanic practices, and raving clients, there are days when earning trust as a Spiritual healer still feels like an uphill climb.

That's why I always encourage people: *consult with a reader or healer before you say yes* to a reading service.

You *do* have intuition. You *can* feel who's right for you, especially in a room full of readers and swirling energies. *Trust your body.*

Here's what I mean: when you approach a reader, pay attention to how you feel in your gut. Do you feel safe? Do you feel like you could sit down and bare your soul? Or do you feel the opposite, that something's just off? That resistance is your intuition speaking. Respect it. If you wouldn't go to coffee with that person, why would you hand them access to your deepest questions?

At psychic fairs or metaphysical shows, you may not always get the chance to meet readers beforehand. In those situations, lean on your senses. Observe. Watch how people leave their tables. Do they look uplifted, thoughtful, lighter? Or do they look shaken in a way that feels out of balance? Remember: not all tears are bad tears, sometimes a breakthrough brings tears of release. What you're looking for is alignment: do the people leaving that space seem supported, seen, and steadied?

Before you even step into an event like this, check your own energy. These environments carry a lot of vibration, not necessarily negative, but amplified. If you're empathic, it's easy to get overwhelmed by all the energies in the room. Take breaks. Step outside. Ground yourself before deciding. The clearer you are, the more easily you'll discern what reader is right for you.

This advice extends beyond fairs. If you're booking a one-on-one session or working online, listen to your gut. If something feels off, that's valid.

When things come up and get in the way of booking the appointment, such as it is after-hours, your credit card won't go through, or you lose their business card, that is likely your Guides or Angels stepping in to protect you.

When you find a reader or healer who validates your experiences, who offers information that resonates deeply *and* feels "spot on," celebrate it. That's the resonance you're looking for.

When Everything Goes Sideways

There was a time during my training when I was scheduled to read as part of my coursework. From the very beginning, something felt off. All day, nothing was lining up, I kept losing track of time, and an uneasiness was rising in my chest, making me feel nauseous, almost like panic. By the time the appointment arrived, my booking system glitched and crashed. Then the video platform failed. My client and I simply couldn't connect.

I was ready to reschedule, but she offered her own platform since we had both set aside the time. Befuddled and thrown off, I decided to persevere. And let me tell you, it was the worst reading I've ever completed. Her energy felt murky, blocked, and nothing landed right. For the first time, a client actively blocked and was argumentative about my process, down to the very belief systems I represented. I regret persevering. I believe there were other energies at play that neither of us could have shifted in that moment.

It took me weeks and several meetings with my mentors to find my footing again. But the lesson was priceless: when the signs are stacking against something, I listen. Now, instead of pushing through, no matter what, I reschedule. I allow myself time to step back, clear my head, and ask: *Is this really where I need to be right now?* More importantly, I can take it a step further and kindly identify and decline due to a mismatch in energies.

Since then, following the path of least resistance has opened greater rewards than I could have imagined. Discernment, trusting the signs, honoring the pauses, has become one of the most valuable tools in my practice.

When you receive a reading, make sure you understand the messages. Ask questions. Challenge the interpretation so you can fully understand the merit of the reading. Energy is personal.

For example, I might tell someone I see the color red in their aura. For me, red is strength, vitality, groundedness. But for someone else, red might symbolize anger or fear. The color is just a reference point for me. The meaning is in the message.

In this exact example, it's not really about the color red at all. It's about the *message* the color carries. What matters is that I convey the energy of strength, vitality, and groundedness that came through, not just the symbol or color that delivered it. The color is the vocabulary; the message is the meaning.

Conversely, when I am given a new symbol during a reading, I inquire what that symbol may mean to my client. Often, it is for them, like an inside joke from their Guides, I don't need to understand.

That's what I mean when I say my role isn't to impress, it's to translate energy. My role is to interpret what Source and the Guides show me in a way that resonates with the person in front of me because the same image, sound, or feeling can hold a completely different meaning depending on who's receiving it.

Decoding the Symbols of Source

People often ask: *Why do readers ask so many questions?*

Because sometimes, we don't know what the messages mean, we just *receive* them.

Let me be clear: it is a message for you. I do not need to understand it fully, and Source doesn't "speak in human." So I need to know how it relates to you.

When I receive information, it often comes in symbols that make sense to me but may not to you until we connect the dots. For example, I frequently see locks and keys. That usually represents people who have the resources to unlock their own freedom but need guidance to bring the pieces together. Someone else might see a lock and think of being trapped, or keeping secrets: same symbol, different meaning.

I might see a rocking horse and say, "Does that mean anything to you?" For example, the rocking horse might symbolize childhood joy for one person, while for another, it could represent a real horse. That's not fishing. That's me matching the symbol to *your* experience. I'm not here to impress you; I'm here to translate energy.

That's why I ask questions like, *"Does this make sense?"* Not because I'm unsure of myself, but because I'm making sure the information is landing in a way that resonates with *you.* My role isn't to prove how accurate I am. My role is to take what Source shows me and translate it the way it applies to your journey.

Sometimes the information makes immediate sense, and sometimes it doesn't click until later. I've had clients call me weeks or even months afterward to say, "Now I understand what you meant." The timing doesn't diminish the accuracy; it just means the symbol needed to develop in their own life before it became clear.

That's the sacred work of translation. It's less about performance and more about alignment. My role isn't to give you a perfect picture, it's to open the window so you can see what's waiting to be revealed.

Sometimes, what we see won't make sense in the moment. That's okay. Source speaks in layers, and understanding often arrives after reflection.

I work with individuals to help them learn to recognize and receive their own messages. First, I start with the basics of, "How do you receive? Do you hear? Do you see? Do you smell? Do you taste? Or maybe you just know. Or some combination of those."

Most importantly, you must also recognize that messages from Source do not often arrive in a " human-spoken language." Sometimes that happens... but not frequently. A significant amount of decoding occurs while receiving information. Again, this is why I talk through the messages with my clients for clarity.

Like playing charades, it's best when you understand your teammate.

The Weight of a Word

"Psychic"

"Intuitive"

"Healer"

"Medium"

Each of these words carries baggage, history, and a thousand interpretations. But at their core, they all mean one thing: connection. Connection to Source, to one another, to the unseen threads weaving through our lives and interconnecting the plains of existence.

When I finally stopped caring about which label fit best, I started to feel free. I stopped diluting my language to make others comfortable. I realized that my work didn't need to be justified, it needed to be lived.

Growing up in the Bible Belt taught me to speak the language of realism, even when the words don't match the practice. I've prayed beside Christians, meditated with mystics, practiced rituals with shamans, and held space for skeptics, all with the same intention: healing.

At the end of the day, it's not about who you say you are. It's about what people feel in your presence.

Becoming Fluent in Authenticity

Over time, I've come to see authenticity as a dialect of courage. It's not loud. It's not rebellious. It's simply the unfiltered truth.

And truth, I've learned, vibrates higher than fear.

When you speak it, even quietly, it changes the room.

There will always be people who misunderstand this work, who try to box it into categories they can control. That's okay. The real magic happens when we stop trying to fit in and start going with the flow.

Closing Reflection

Stepping into your gifts publicly requires courage, especially when the environment around you doesn't embrace them. Whether in the Bible Belt or a boardroom, there is always risk in being transparent about your intuitive nature. Yet each time we choose authenticity over hiding, we permit others to do the same.

Journal Prompt

Reflect on a time when you felt out of place because of who you are or what you believe. How did you navigate that? What would you say now to your younger self in that moment?

____

____

____

____

____

____

____

____

____

Chapter 3

✳

"Woo" on Pause

Healing may not be so much about getting
better, as about letting go of
everything that isn't you.
Rachel Naomi Remen

There was a season when I put my gifts on the shelf. Not because I stopped believing in them, but because life got loud. Education. Marriage. Motherhood. Mortgages. The practical, everyday things that demanded attention, whether my spirit was awake or not.

After a few years of chasing the metaphysical circuit, traveling eight, ten, sometimes twelve hours one way just to set up at a show, the chapter of my life as a weekend psychic reader and vendor came to a close.

The reasons were both practical and personal. The profits were slim, my aunt's marriage was unraveling, and I was preparing for a new marriage of my own. With a bonus daughter in my life, weekends on the road no longer made sense.

Motherhood brought a different rhythm. I continued my career in social work, and when I look back now, I see clearly that intuition was my strongest tool in that field. Textbooks didn't rebuild families after a crisis; intuition did; reading what was said and unsaid, and guiding treatment plans that fit each unique situation.

I was no longer being "paid" for my intuitive services. I wasn't setting up booths, reading cards, or scanning handwriting. I was living everyday life, quietly weaving intuition into it without giving it full acknowledgment as my gift at work.

When I became pregnant with my youngest, I faced another crossroads. Human services work would not afford me the kind of relationship with my child that I wanted. I couldn't see myself sending my newborn child to daycare while I helped other families achieve safety and stability.

Leaving this career in human services was one of the hardest choices of my life, because I felt highly rewarded making a difference. There was fear and so much self-doubt about being a mom, starting over, finding my place, and leaving the "comfort" of my career to follow my heart and the desire to be a mother, present with her child.

I took a massive leap of faith. I bought a "turnkey" sign business. There, among ink, graphics, and marketing projects, my daughter was raised without daycare, without babysitters, just us together, growing. Employees also needed to serve in the shared "parenting" role with my children. My business was a safe haven, a homework stop, and an after-school hang-out for their children and grandchildren, too.

Intuition in Business, Intuition in Family

Looking back, I see that my intuition never left me; it just showed up in new ways.

In the sign business, when customers described their vision, I didn't just hear their words; I *felt* them. Their passion, their excitement, their urgency flowed into me. If they were unsure or scattered, I would sometimes "hold" their vision for them until it came into clarity.

There were times when a customer described a project so vividly that I could see it fully formed in my mind, as if it were already printed and installed. Other times, they left me with vague impressions, and I would "sleep on it." In the dream state, the design would arrive whole and complete. I'd wake up with a picture in my mind, ready to bring it into the world.

I remember one client who came in, stressed and overwhelmed, saying only, "We need something bold, something that makes people stop and notice." They had no colors, no fonts, no imagery in mind. That night, I dreamed of a sign in bright cobalt blue with stark white lettering, clean and modern, commanding attention. I designed it the next morning, and when they saw it, they exclaimed, "That's exactly what we needed."

Another customer, a small-town café owner, came in with hand-scribbled notes on napkins and scraps of paper. We chatted about "warmth," "home," and "the smell of fresh coffee." As they spoke, I could almost *taste* what they were describing. I created a rustic logo with earthy tones, steam rising from a coffee cup shaped like a heart. They cried when they saw it. "You got me," they said.

This wasn't graphic design alone; it was energy work, translated into form.

The Slow Drift Away

I used to think that losing connection to my intuition was failure. Now I know it's just part of the rhythm. We ebb and flow. We expand and contract. Sometimes our gifts need rest, too.

With my oldest daughter, I was laser-focused on keeping her world steady. Routine, security, predictability, all the things I never felt as a kid. In doing so, I quieted the part of myself that thrives on spontaneity, mystery, and movement.

I became the "responsible one." The woman with a planner, a job, and a label-maker. I laughed less, created less, and played less. But I was surviving, and that felt like enough.

Then one day, I caught myself watching her color outside the lines. And something in me cracked wide open. She was fearless with those crayons, purple trees, orange cats, blue grass, and it hit me: somewhere along the way, I'd traded in wonder for order.

That realization hurt in the best possible way. It reminded me that I hadn't lost my gifts; *I'd just forgotten how to play.*

A Mother's Intuition

My youngest daughter's gifts emerged early. Even as an infant nursing in the middle of the night, she was distracted by entities drawn to her light. I often had to tell them, "Not now. You may return when she is finished." By age three, she was learning to dowse, what many in the Midwest would recognize as water witching, using a simple paperclip tied to a string. Dowsing is a way of asking simple yes or no questions and allowing subtle movement to respond, sometimes called pendulum work. "Paper clip, paper clip..." she would whisper, watching it sway with certainty. Children don't doubt magic. They live in it. Too often, that ability is educated out of them.

Her older sister also began to show her gifts, particularly in her sensitivity to stones and crystals, echoing my own visceral response to amber. Together, we practiced small, playful exercises that helped them explore their intuition, grounding them in the understanding that we are souls having a human experience.

One of those exercises was creating what we called balls of white light. This is simply a way of learning how to notice and perceive energy. It often begins by removing distractions, rubbing the hands together to feel warmth and sensation, then holding them as if cradling a small sphere. Some people imagine light or movement there. Others feel a gentle pulsing or simply sense that something is present. There is no right way. The practice helps you recognize how *you* receive information, whether through seeing, feeling, or knowing.

The girls took to this easily. They treated it like play, letting the energy expand or soften, learning to focus without force. When we were finished, we expressed gratitude and allowed the energy to return, sometimes bringing it back into the body as a way of restoring calm and balance. It was never about creating something extraordinary, only about noticing what was already there.

One of my proudest moments came when my youngest described how she'd calmed herself before a test at school. She had gone into the restroom, cleared her energetic field, and quieted her nerves. I had always felt nervous in school settings myself, so to see her equipped with tools I hadn't known as a child was a gift to witness.

Creativity Rekindled

Intuition continued to show up in other ways. Floating became my sanctuary. In the theta brainwave state of deep relaxation, my creativity flowed unhindered. Designs, ideas, and inspirations came rushing in.

I want to clarify that my reference to "floating, or the float" is about floatation therapy. Floatation is a therapeutic experience where the body is suspended effortlessly in a warm, high-salinity environment, allowing the nervous system to shift into deep parasympathetic rest. With external stimulation minimized, the brain finally has space to down-regulate, process, and recalibrate. It is less about luxury and more about giving the mind and body uninterrupted neurological recovery.

I discovered it while searching for management of chronic pain, stress, and insomnia. It has evolved into a business. As I grew more aware, my float practice has taken on a greater role in my physical, mental, and spiritual well-being.

Quieting the mind chatter was a significant step toward reuniting with my intuition and Source. The weight of being a business owner, mother, and wife all too often perpetuated the chatter. Floating was a significant tool in helping me learn to quiet the chatter and to appreciate the silence. At first, the thought of being alone with my thoughts and the chatter was daunting. Now, I look forward to the silence that I can achieve on my own without needing to float. Ten years later, I still find that floats spark my clearest bursts of creation and reconnection with Source.

The Flea Market Awakening

My true spiritual reawakening came unexpectedly at a local fall flea market.

It was a dusty day at the fairgrounds, with every booth packed with antiques, trinkets, and treasures. I was drawn to a wooden sewing machine and cabinet. The moment I touched it, I felt and saw the quilts pieced together, the clothes repaired, the pride of the woman who once used it. The energy of her devotion was still alive in this machine.

Then I spotted a cedar chest. In my family, it was tradition to give a hope chest for graduation, and I thought this would be perfect for my daughter, who was about to graduate from high school. But as I stepped into its energy and touched the wood, tears came. These weren't my tears; they were the tears of memories and lives lived with that chest. My body trembled. I knew this was not the energy to carry forward into my daughter's future.

These experiences reminded me: my connection was back. Fully alive. And with it came a new responsibility: boundaries. The boundaries I had learned through the months of active healing preceding this awakening. I would need these boundaries to stop the cycle, stay whole and true to my path.

That was my reawakening.

Not a lightning bolt. Not a breakdown. Just a quiet, undeniable knowing that my gifts were still there, waiting for me to come home. Waiting for the next level of BEING.

Boundaries and Respect

The sewing machine, the cedar chest, even estate jewelry, objects carry imprints. Sometimes the energy is joyful, while at other times it is heavy or unresolved. I've learned to celebrate the positive and to let go of what no longer serves, honoring those who have left their mark.

This chapter of my life, the pause from public "woo," the years of family, business, and everyday living, taught me that intuition never really leaves. It may be quiet. It may change form. But it waits for us, ready to be reignited, when we are prepared to step forward again.

Reawakening Your Purpose

Reawakening your gifts isn't just about remembering what you can do; it's about unlearning the fear of being seen doing it. For so long, I'd stayed quiet to stay safe. But as I began opening back up, I realized that fear wasn't protecting me anymore; it was suffocating me.

It's a strange paradox, isn't it? We spend years shutting down our intuition to fit in, and then one day we ache to get it back.

That ache is the soul's alarm clock. When you can no longer tolerate the dullness of pretending, that's when the real awakening begins.

The fear doesn't vanish overnight. It dissolves in layers, as you learn to trust your intuition again, your signals, your sense of truth.

For me, it started with small moments: telling a friend about a hunch that turned out to be right, journaling my feelings without editing, and allowing myself to believe what I sensed.

Every time I honored that truth, my intuition grew louder.

Every time I ignored it, I felt hollow.

Eventually, I couldn't un-hear it anymore.

Finding Wholeness in Pause

Putting my gifts on pause wasn't failure, it was integration. It was learning to live as a human first, healer second.

Because the truth is, your spiritual awakening doesn't erase your humanity; it anchors it. The pause, the stillness, the so-called lull, isn't wasted time. It's compost. Everything you think you've buried is actually feeding your next bloom.

When I finally re-emerged, I didn't come back as the same woman who had gone quiet. I came back with roots deeper and stronger than before. This time, I knew better than to trade wonder for order again.

Closing Reflection: When Your "Woo" Feels on Pause

There will be seasons when your gifts feel quiet. When life demands your attention elsewhere, family, career, or survival, you may believe your intuition has slipped away. But it never leaves you.

Your "woo" is patient. It waits in the background, woven into everyday choices, conversations, and creative sparks. It reveals itself in dreams, in sudden clarity, in the love you pour into your children or your work. When the time is right, it rises again, sometimes in unexpected places, like a flea market or a float pod.

If your gifts feel muted, don't despair. Honor the pause. Live the season you are in. Trust that intuition, once awakened, is never lost. It will return to you, fuller and deeper, when you are ready to welcome it again.

Journal Prompt

Take a moment to reflect on a season of your life when your intuition felt quiet, or perhaps even absent.

What was happening for you during that time, and how did it shape the way you showed up in your daily life?

As you look back now, can you see ways your inner knowing was still present, even if subtle, through dreams, small nudges, or creative bursts?

Write about the wisdom that particular "pause" gave you, and how it may have prepared you for the return of your gifts in a fuller, deeper way.

____

____

____

____

____

____

____

____

Chapter 4

This Isn't My Life... and How I Changed It

I am not what happened to me,
I am what I choose to become.
Carl Jung

In my first book, *Blooming Into Life*, I shared pieces of my story. What I didn't fully share was just how far out of alignment I really was.

Not just tired. Not just stressed.

I'm talking about waking up every day with dread in my chest, resenting the life I had created, and feeling like I was sleepwalking through my own existence.

I didn't want to keep doing "more of this."

That's the real sign, by the way. You don't have to know exactly what you want, but when you know what you *don't* want, when the thought of "more of this" makes your stomach churn, you're ready for change.

The Basement of the Lighthouse

I was angry. Bitter. I felt like people were taking advantage of me, especially at my lowest.

Recently divorced. Mid-pandemic. The world felt upside down. And me? Lost in a fog so thick I couldn't see the path in front of me.

That's when I stumbled into ThetaHealing® and met the woman who would become my coach. In one of our first sessions, she told me she saw me in a lighthouse.

This is how she reads people, seeing them in a lighthouse. She relates where they are in their personal lighthouse of life.

In my lighthouse, I was not at the top, casting light. Not even on the main floor. Where was I? In the basement, surrounded by the stagnation of sludge and debris, unable to climb out.

And she was right.

When she described it, something inside me broke open. I could *feel* the sludge, the weight of every choice I'd made out of fear, guilt, or survival.

The smell of stagnation. The panic that someone could see what I'd been hiding even from myself. It was raw, sticky, and honest.

I remember thinking, "This is gross. I don't like it. But it's true." For the first time, someone had mirrored back not my potential, but my pain. Somehow, that truth was its own kind of grace.

I recall the feeling of desolation, being beaten down and completely defeated as Dr. Tanya described the sludge-filled basement of my lighthouse. The actual physical sense of stagnation and being sunk deep in a quagmire. The panic of realizing someone can see what I feel.

It was gross in there. Heavy. Suffocating. I didn't like it. Yet I couldn't deny it. Her words hit me in my gut with full force: I was trapped.

That moment was brutal. But it was also the beginning.

The work began. And with it came not just healing, but rather, awakening.

Awakening is not a gentle process.

The Anger That Comes With Waking Up

When you start reconnecting with yourself, you begin to see how much of your life you've been living on autopilot. You see that the "normal" you've been sold isn't your normal at all.

When you start reconnecting with yourself, there is often a moment, sometimes quiet, sometimes explosive, when you realize just how long you have been living on autopilot. You begin to see the places where you abandoned your truth to keep the peace, wore masks to survive, or silenced yourself because that was what was modeled for you. With that awareness can come anger. Real, bodily anger.

It's the anger of discovering that the "normal" you were handed was never *your* normal. The anger of seeing how much of your life was shaped by expectations you never consciously agreed to. The anger that rises when you realize how many decisions were shaped by fear, conditioning, or compliance, rather than by who you truly are.

For some, this anger feels like betrayal, like the influences that shaped you acted as unintentional traitors to your soul. Even if no one meant harm, the result can feel the same: you were shaped by forces that never took *you* into account.

And so you begin to ask the questions you were never allowed to ask: *Whose story have I been living? Who taught me to shrink? Who decided what was acceptable for me? Who benefited from my silence?*

This is where your awakening begins, not in light and ease, but in the raw honesty of naming what has held you back.

You realize you've been living inside a story written for you by...

Family expectations:

Many of us discover that we have been living inside a story shaped long before we ever had a chance to question it. Family expectations often become invisible scripts, how we "should" behave, what roles we are expected to fill, or who we are allowed to become. These patterns aren't usually malicious; they are inherited ways of surviving, belonging, or keeping the peace. But when those expectations conflict with our inner truth, they can quietly limit our ability to choose differently. Healing begins when we recognize which parts of our story were handed to us and which ones we are free to rewrite.

Cultural conditioning:

Culture creates a framework for how we interpret the world, but it can also become a cage when its assumptions go unexamined. Cultural conditioning teaches us what is acceptable, what is "normal," and what parts of ourselves must stay hidden to remain included. Sometimes these messages are subtle, passed through jokes, expectations, and unspoken rules. Other times, they are blunt and enforced. Becoming aware of this conditioning allows us to see where we've minimized ourselves to fit in, and it opens the awareness of choosing alignment over compliance.

Social expectations:

From a young age, we absorb the social expectations of the communities around us. We learn what is valued, what is judged, and what earns approval. Many people don't realize how much of their adult life is shaped by the desire to be accepted, to not disappoint, to not draw attention, to not break the rules. This kind of social pressure can cause us to shrink, overperform, or silence our intuition to maintain harmony. Healing invites us to step back and ask: "Is this truly who I am, or who I've been trained to be?"

The Midwest way of keeping everyone polite and predictable.

Growing up in the Midwest often means being raised with a deep respect for kindness, humility, and not rocking the boat. These values can be beautiful, but they can also teach us to soften our truth, keep our gifts quiet, and avoid anything that feels too bold, emotional, or unusual. Many intuitives learn early that their sensitivities don't fit neatly into the safe, predictable boxes that Midwest culture prefers. Naming this dynamic isn't about judgment; it's about understanding why stepping into your authentic self can feel like an act of rebellion, even when it is simply an act of honesty.

Old beliefs picked up from religion, school, and workplaces.

Beliefs gathered from religion, school, or professional environments often become internalized long before we understand how they shape us. These systems can give structure, meaning, and community, but they can also instill fear, shame, perfectionism, or self-doubt. Many people carry outdated beliefs about worth, morality, or success that no longer serve their present life. Part of intuitive healing is gently examining these inherited frameworks and releasing the ones that keep us small or disconnected from our inner knowing.

Ancestral traditions, brought along for the ride.

We don't just inherit eye color or mannerisms, we inherit stories, traumas, strengths, and coping patterns from the generations that came before us. Ancestral traditions can offer grounding and wisdom; yet they can also carry unfinished emotional or energetic imprints. Sometimes we live out responses that aren't ours simply because they were passed down as survival strategies. Acknowledging ancestral influence allows us to hold compassion for what our lineage endured while choosing which patterns to keep and which to release as we step into our story.

Here's the hard part: realizing that most of the people who shaped that story weren't trying to hurt you. They were trying to help. They handed you the best version of truth they had access to. *But it was their truth, filtered through their fears, their conditioning, their survival strategies, not yours.*

Let me tell you, anger is a natural part of this process. I remember sitting in a staff meeting at work, biting my tongue as someone else took credit for an idea I had spent hours developing. I smiled, nodded, and "stayed professional." But inside, I was seething. At the time, I thought the anger meant I was being petty or overly sensitive. Later, I realized it was my intuition screaming: *This is a boundary violation.* It wasn't about the meeting. It was about every moment in my life where I had been conditioned to swallow my voice, play small, be agreeable, be grateful, be quiet, be "nice."

That one moment revealed the entire pattern.

That's how awakening often begins, not with fireworks or spiritual clarity, but with irritation, resentment, a sudden discomfort you can no longer explain away. Anger becomes the flashlight that shines into the corners you've been trained not to look into. It shows you where you've been overridden, overlooked, or taught to override yourself.

You start to see all the places where your boundaries were never modeled... where your emotions were minimized... where your gifts were dismissed... where your truth was treated as an inconvenience rather than a compass.

This can be disorienting. You may feel betrayed by the very systems, communities, or people you trusted. You might look back at relationships, jobs, commitments, and wonder, *Why did I tolerate that? Why didn't I speak up? Why did I think this was normal?* It's easy to turn that anger inward but let me be clear: These responses were not failures. They were adaptations. You were surviving a story you didn't yet know you were allowed to question.

As this clarity emerges, the anger doesn't just point to what hurt you, it points to what matters to you. It shows you where your values live. It marks the places where your boundaries want to grow. It reveals the parts of you that are finally ready to come home.

This is the moment where the old story begins to lose its hold. This is where your nervous system starts whispering, *No more.* This is where your soul says, *My truth deserves a turn.*

And once you see the difference between the story you inherited and the story that is authentically yours, you cannot unsee it. The awakening has already begun. The anger is simply the spark that lights the way forward.

Now you get to decide what stays, what heals, and what you are finally ready to release.

Being a social worker, I saw people with problems. I didn't see the kinds of parents who raise healthy, happy kids. What I did see was that new parents tended to swing too far in the opposite direction from how they were raised:

Strict parents produce lax parents.

When someone grows up under rigid rules, constant monitoring, or harsh discipline, they often remember how small and powerless that felt. So when they become parents, they vow, quietly or out loud, *I will never make my child feel like that.* In an effort to undo the pain they experienced, they loosen the reins too far. They mistake permissiveness for love because structure once felt like control. Their parenting becomes a reaction, not a reflection of what their child truly needs.

Lax parents produce strict ones.

On the other side, individuals who grew up without guidance, routine, or accountability often feel lost in adulthood. There were no guardrails, no clear expectations, no reliable structure to lean on. So when they become parents, they tighten down with rules, schedules, and consequences, sometimes excessively. They are not trying to be controlling; they are trying to create the stability they never had. But again, the pendulum swings too far, driven by fear rather than intention.

Few are finding balance. How could they? They didn't know how.

Most families aren't failing out of carelessness; they're repeating patterns they never examined. Balance is hard to practice when it was never modeled. Parenting becomes a form of emotional inheritance, shaped by unmet needs, unhealed wounds, and good intentions wrapped in old survival strategies. Without awareness, the pendulum keeps swinging, generation after generation. Healing begins when someone finally pauses long enough to ask: *What does my child actually need, and what am I reacting to from my own past?*

We repeat or reject but rarely reflect.

I had to accept that my upbringing, while well-intentioned, didn't meet my actual needs. That doesn't make my family villains, it just makes them human. Still... it hurt to realize that my life, as I'd been living it, wasn't *mine.*

All the well-intended adults with their own values and ideas molded me into who I have become. By social standards, I had become a good, thoughtful, and nurturing human. But I had to question what was really right for me. At the root of it all, I was unhappy and just going through the same day-to-day motions.

The Prescribed Life

By my mid to late 40s, I could see it clearly:

I'd been following a prescription I didn't write. Widowhood. Social work. Parenting by the book (sometimes *society's* book, not mine). Holding jobs where I bit my tongue. Staying small to avoid rocking the boat.

As a child, staying small kept me safe. As an adult, it kept me invisible. I had been praised for being capable, responsible, and kind. But no one had ever asked if I was happy. Truthfully, I hadn't asked myself either. I didn't know it was a choice…

 I let people walk over me because I didn't know I could set boundaries about *anything*.

Here's the truth: That anger you feel? Nine times out of ten, it's from someone violating a boundary you didn't even know you had.

I had built a beautiful cage. It looked like success from the outside: home, family, stability. But inside, I was crumbling.

It's crushing to realize that the life you fought for is actually the thing you need to leave behind.

The Breaking Point

When you wake up and realize, "*This isn't my life,*" it's terrifying.

Most of the time, you can't even see it until you're out of it.

You need a coach, a trusted friend, someone to point it out while you're still in the thick of it.

For me, that wake-up call came in waves, small moments that built into one undeniable truth: I was done performing my life.

I was done decorating the lighthouse's basement. I wanted to climb to the top and turn the damn light back on.

The breaking point came one quiet night in my kitchen. The dishes were stacked high, the house was silent, and I was standing there staring at a sink full of soapy water, thinking, "Is this it? Is this really all my life will ever be?"

That night, I cried harder than I had in years. But when I wiped those tears, I made a decision: I was done living a life that drained me dry.

Then comes the hard part: deciding what *I want instead*.

It's a crushing, mind-bending moment to see that the "truth" you've lived by was never your own. That which you thought was normal was not. That the people you thought would protect you sometimes couldn't or wouldn't.

Yet, that realization, that gut-punch of honesty, is where the magic begins. Because once you see it, you can't unsee it. That's the exact moment the rebuilding starts. Often, this realization feels like a massive setback in life as we know it. Sit with it. Celebrate the new vision you have gained. Your future is likely still unknown, but rest assured, it will be brighter and of your own making.

How to Get Out of the Cycle

People ask me all the time: *How do you change it? How do you break free from the cycle?*

Although it's different for everyone, there are some universal steps that everyone must take.

Step one: Decide you don't want the cycle anymore. We can gripe and complain about our lives all day long, but if that's where our focus stays, we just get more of it. What you resist, persists.

Step two: Look for gratitude like your life depends on it, because it does. Not fake positivity. Not bypassing the hard stuff. But the willingness to find one small glimmer of light in the darkness. And then another.

When I was at my lowest point, I started a "three glimmers" practice.

Every night before bed, I wrote down three things that didn't completely suck that day.

Some nights it was as simple as "good coffee, my daughter's laugh, didn't cry in the car."

But over time, I began to find beauty in places I'd never looked before.

I began noticing the flower beds in my neighborhood, not just as landscaping, but as quiet love offerings from people I'd never met. I found myself taking different routes home just to admire the care someone had taken to arrange their irises, and the way vines climbed fences as if they had something to say.

I started seeing color, texture, and intention in places I used to overlook. The chipped paint on a porch swing told a story. The rust on an old gate glinted gold in the sunlight. Even the way someone had folded a blanket on their porch made me feel tender, as if it were waiting for someone they loved.

I began to hear the rhythm of the world again: wind chimes in the distance, birds announcing morning, the crunch of gravel beneath someone's boots. It was like the world had always been whispering, and for the first time in a long time... I had turned toward it.

These things had always been there. But I hadn't been there, *not like this.*

Gratitude is the flashlight that helps you find the door out of the cycle.

I picture practicing gratitude like walking on a beach. At first, all you see is trash and broken shells. But if you keep looking, you start spotting small pebbles you like. Then a bigger stone. Then a beautiful, perfect shell.

The beauty was always there; you just weren't looking for it... at first.

Here's the kicker: manifesting doesn't happen by sitting in front of a vision board while bingeing Netflix. Manifesting, at its core, is about learning to think, feel, and act as if what you desire is already in motion. It's not about pretending or hoping. It's about alignment. That is manifestation.

It happens when you start living like you believe you're worth more.

Step Three: Take one small action that aligns with the life you actually want. Awareness without action keeps you stuck in the same room with the lights on. At some point, you have to move. Not with grand gestures or dramatic reinventions, those usually collapse under the weight of expectation. I'm talking about one small step that signals to your nervous system, *We are doing this differently now.*

Maybe it's saying no to something you usually agree to out of obligation. Maybe it's cleaning one drawer, not the whole house. Maybe it's sending the email you've been avoiding. Maybe it's putting your shoes by the door because you want to take a walk tomorrow, even if you don't trust yourself to actually go.

The size of the action doesn't matter. Its alignment does. Your system needs evidence, tangible, lived proof, that you are no longer just thinking about change, you are participating in it. That one step becomes the bridge between intention and embodiment.

Step Four: Become radically honest about what is no longer sustainable. This is the step most people try to skip, because it asks you to face what you've been tolerating. Tolerating is a quiet kind of self-abandonment. When you finally pause long enough to ask, *What isn't working anymore?* the answers often come faster than you expect.

Maybe it's a relationship you've outgrown. Maybe it's a belief you inherited but never questioned. Maybe it's the exhaustion you keep calling "normal." Maybe it's the role you play in your family that no longer fits the person you are becoming.

Radical honesty is not about blame, it's about clarity. It's the moment you stop gaslighting yourself into staying small. It's the moment you say, "This version of my life may have protected me once, but it cannot carry me forward."

Yes, this honesty may stir grief, anger, or fear. That's okay. Those emotions are not signs of failure; they are signs of awakening.

When you name what is no longer sustainable, you release the anchor that's been keeping you tied to a shoreline you've already outgrown.

Once you've reached this point, once you've decided to break the cycle, practiced gratitude until you could see in the dark, taken one aligned step, and told the truth about what no longer fits, you are no longer repeating the story you inherited. You are writing a new one. The world inside you shifts. Slowly at first, then unmistakably.

This is where real change begins: at the intersection of awareness, gratitude, action, and honesty.

Manifesting the Life That's Actually Yours

Once you start finding those small pieces of good, you can begin to *design*.

Ask yourself:
What does my perfect day look like?
What qualities do I want in my closest friends?
What kind of partner do I want beside me?

Write it down.
Speak it.
Feel it.

Manifestation isn't about wishing, it's about alignment of your energy. You start matching your energy to the life you're creating. That's why the Universe listens so closely when you stop complaining and start imagining.

When you focus solely on what you *want*, you send a clear message to the Universe. You flip the script from resentment to creation.

The negative people? They'll drift away, because they don't like your new frequency. And you won't like the feel of theirs either.

Your circle naturally changes. Your opportunities change. You start attracting what actually belongs to you. What makes you feel whole and brings you joy?

This Is How You Do It

Not by wishing life were different. Not by waiting for someone to rescue you.

But by waking up, telling the truth, and choosing, every day, to collect the pieces of beauty, hope, and possibility until they outweigh the debris.

This is how *you* build *your* life. The one you came here to live.

This is not luck. It's alignment. When you choose to live from truth instead of survival, life starts meeting you halfway.

From Survival to Sovereignty

Healing isn't about becoming a "new" version of yourself. It's about remembering who you were before the world told you who to be.

It's about reclaiming the fragments you scattered while trying to belong.

When I finally climbed out of that lighthouse basement, I didn't emerge polished or perfect. I came out muddy, shaky, and still unsure, but I was free.

Freedom, I've learned, is worth every scraped knee and every burned bridge.

Closing Reflection

There comes a moment when the weight of living someone else's story becomes unbearable. The roles, the expectations, the beliefs we inherited, all of it begins to feel like a cage.

That moment of reckoning, as painful as it is, is also a doorway. By choosing to question, to release, and to dream again, we begin to create a life that is truly our own.

Change doesn't come from knowing every next step. It begins with one courageous truth:

This isn't my life.

Journal Prompt

Take a deep breath and ask yourself:

What do I want *my* life to look like? Doing what? With whom in it?

Where in my life am I living according to someone else's rules, expectations, or story?

Write honestly about what feels misaligned.

Then, imagine your life if you were free from those obligations, what would your days look like, feel like, sound like?

Let your pen sketch the beginnings of your own story.

____

____

____

____

____

____

____

____

____

Part Two:

Becoming Who You're Meant to Be

Chapter 5 — I Have Always Had My Gifts... So What?
Shadow work, soul work, and stepping into your
authentic power without apology.

Chapter 6 — The Transparency Tension
Coming out as an intuitive in a world that doesn't always
understand—and learning to feel safe in your truth.

Chapter 7 — The Cycles of Emergence
The sacred rhythm of retreating, recharging, and
re-emerging as your energy evolves.

Chapter 5

I Have Always Had
My Gifts… So What?

You don't need fixing.
You need remembering — remembering who you
truly are beneath the programming.
Rebecca Campbell

I've always known things. Not in the "I'm a genius" way, but in that deep-belly knowing that comes without proof.

Since I was little, I could sense moods, shifts, changes before anyone said a word. If someone were sad, I'd feel it in my own chest. If someone were angry, it would rattle my whole body.

At first, I thought everyone was like this. Didn't everyone's skin prickle before bad news came? Didn't everyone feel the heaviness in a room before a fight broke out?

Apparently not.

It took me years, decades, honestly, to realize that this wasn't how everyone else experienced the world.

Learning My Normal

I used to joke that I was "emotionally porous." But that's really what it felt like, like I had no filter over what comes to me. Other people's emotions would roll in like weather fronts.

If I walked into a campus, I'd get dizzy from all the energy. Crowded stores made me anxious. Even someone sitting next to me on a plane could leave me drained if they were carrying grief or fear.

Back then, I didn't have language for any of this. I just knew that sometimes I needed to hide in my car after being around too many people.

Music helped. Baths helped. Silence helped most of all.

But of course, life doesn't let you stay in silence for long. I had jobs to do, children to raise, and people depending on me. So I learned to cope by pushing my gifts down and rationalizing the rest.

The problem with ignoring your gifts is that they don't go away, they just start leaking out sideways.

For me, it looked like anxiety and depression. Fatigue. A constant low hum of irritation.

The Moment of Realization

It wasn't until my midlife unraveling, the one we talked about in the last chapter, that I started seeing the pattern clearly. My gifts had never been the problem. The problem was my resistance to them.

I had spent years trying to fit my knowing into a socially acceptable container. Call it "good instincts," "women's intuition," "empathy."

Anything but psychic.

Anything but healer.

Anything that wouldn't get me labeled "woo" in the grocery store parking lot.

But suppression doesn't equal safety. It equals stagnation. When you bury your truth to keep the peace, you end up warring with yourself.

Gifts Don't Expire

The good news? Your gifts wait for you. They're patient. They'll whisper, nudge, or shout, whatever it takes to bring you back.

I sometimes picture mine like loyal dogs waiting at the door. They don't scold when I've been gone too long. They just wag their tails when I finally show up again.

Every time I've returned to my intuitive work, it's been richer, deeper, and more grounded. Because I've lived more. I've learned more.

And living, really living, makes you a better healer.

The world doesn't need perfect practitioners. It requires honest ones.

Rekindling Gifts

Rekindling my gifts was, in itself, a gift. Each obstacle in my life became an invitation to dig deeper, to reconnect with who I truly am, not the woman molded by family, friends, or society's expectations. Not just the EMT, the college graduate, the dyslexic, the social worker, the volunteer, the widow, the wife, the mother, the business owner, or the divorcée.

*But **Amanda Beth**.*

I have always been learning, always curious, always reaching for more. Looking back, I can see that every obstacle was pushing me closer to answering the call of my soul.

At the time, my divorce felt like the absolute end of me.

In hindsight, it was.

It was the end of the person I had been molded into, the one who ran headlong into "doing all the things." The house, the career, the car, the marriage, the children.

On paper, we were perfect. From the outside, we looked whole. Inside, I was dying. I hated being me.

The divorce cracked that shell wide open. Not because it caused the problem, but because it brought everything to the surface at once. It showed me just how deeply I had organized my life around meeting expectations, often at the expense of my own inner truth. By the time the marriage ended, I was at the lowest point I had ever known, stripped of the structures I had relied on and forced to look honestly at how little sovereignty I felt in my own life.

That breaking point became an invitation. Not an easy one, and not one I accepted quickly. It took years to reach a level of pain that outweighed my fear of change. But with the support of a coach, I began to see beyond the terror of uncertainty. I started to recognize how many choices I had made to keep the peace, to hold everything together, and to live in ways that felt acceptable to others rather than true to myself.

The divorce didn't take anything from me. It revealed something. It gave me the opportunity to ask a question I had never fully asked before: Who am I living for? Once that question surfaced, there was no unseeing it. That was where the real change began.

I couldn't "see the future," but I could feel the stagnation of my status quo. I knew I couldn't keep living this way. Whatever lay ahead had to be better than the drain of pretending. Taking that first step of courage to believe life was meant to be lived, loved, and embraced.

Stepping Into Power

What came next wasn't a personality makeover; it was a reclamation. Not louder, truer. Not harder, cleaner. I stopped auditioning for a life I didn't want and began choosing the one that chose me.

This is stepping into your power: not dominance, not performance, not "bitch mode." Power is what remains when the mold breaks and your soul is still standing. It looks like telling the truth kindly, setting clear boundaries without apology, and choosing alignment over approval.

For me, it wasn't flashy. It was the quiet, consistent courage to stop performing the life everyone expected, and start living the one I could actually inhabit. Unapologetic. Bold. Authentic. Not over others, over my own fear.

Red flags you're in performance mode:

You feel resentful after saying yes. Resentment is often the first sign your "yes" wasn't honest. It's the emotional residue left behind when your body already knew the truth, but your mouth couldn't follow through. That resentment isn't pettiness, it's your intuition tapping you on the shoulder, showing you where you've betrayed yourself.

You need others to "get it" before you act. When you're performing, you wait for validation or understanding before making a move. You want someone to cosign your intuition because you don't trust your own knowing yet. This is the hallmark of living out someone else's script.

You over-give, then feel empty. Performance mode makes you pour out more than you have, hoping your effort will earn you love, safety, or acceptance. But over-giving always ends the same way: depletion, frustration, and the quiet ache of feeling unseen despite all you've done.

Your body tightens when you decide. Your body knows when a decision isn't aligned. The tension, the bracing, the tightening, those are early warning systems, not flaws. Performance forces you to override them, but the body never lies.

Green flags you're in your power:

You feel calm after saying no. A true, aligned "no" creates space. You can feel the nervous system settle, the breath deepen, the mind quiet. Calm is the signature of an authentic boundary.

You choose alignment over being liked. When you're in your power, being understood becomes less important than being true. Approval loses its shine, and alignment becomes the only measure that matters.

You take action without over-explaining. Power removes the need to justify your choices. You act because it feels right, not because anyone else approves. Your decisions become statements, not negotiations.

Your body exhales when you make a decision. The body relaxes when truth is chosen. That exhale is not just physical; it's spiritual confirmation that you've returned to yourself.

When you step into your soul's power, you release judgment, of yourself and of others. You rise closer to wholeness, closer to your actual ascension.

This is not "bitch mode." It is soul mode.

I remember working with one particular client who had a significant lifelong history of abuse in many forms. She continued into her life as the caretaker of many, including her abusers. We worked on forgiveness, and establishing boundaries she could manage.

After just a few sessions, she reported having the confidence to stand her ground with a family member. She told me about the conversation and how empowered she felt to state her needs and stick with her boundaries, noting that she was not mean or hateful. She said she was rather shocked by her own level of calm.

This level of empowerment was monumental. But not in the loud, forceful, ego-driven way the world often defines power. This was different. It was the kind of empowerment that comes from within, from soul mode. The deep, quiet knowing that I was finally steering my life instead of bracing for it.

I wasn't trying to control everything; I was choosing with intention. I was no longer outsourcing my worth, waiting for permission, or trying to make myself smaller so others could feel comfortable. I had entered a new rhythm; one led by resonance rather than reaction. This was soul-aligned power: fierce, compassionate, grounded, and fully mine.

I have witnessed this exact scenario play out time and time again. Once a person dares to break the pattern and establishes healthy boundaries they can hold; those who once bullied them are left speechless, the energetic exchange balances.

Circles Change

When you choose alignment, your life rearranges to match it, and your circle is always the first to move.

When you grow, your circle shifts.

Your best friend from kindergarten may no longer be your best friend, not because of dislike, but because you've both changed. As adults, we accept this shift when our friendships narrow into those who truly resonate. On the Spirit-led path, it's the same, except the change often feels more personal, more tender.

At times, growth feels lonely. Healing changes your frequency, and your old circle may not understand. They may just fade away, or they may fight against the new you with statements such as, "You've changed" (and they mean in a not-so-good way), or "Why can't you just be the way you used to be?" Statements like these might feel hurtful at first, until you realize what they really are: an indicator that you are growing. Remember, these are statements from, and about those who want to keep the "Old you" they were comfortable with.

Soon, those who resonate with your new vibration, and mirror the truth of who you are, become your circle.

They don't just feel like home, they show up like it.

They call just because you crossed their mind. They invite you on spontaneous outings with no agenda except to be together. There's no list to accomplish, no performance to uphold, just shared presence, laughter, and the sacred simplicity of doing "nothing" and having it mean everything.

You go for drives with no destination. You linger over coffee until it becomes dinner. You celebrate small wins with candlelight, and big belly laughs. You talk about energy, dreams, ancestors, the mundane, the mystical, and nothing is off limits.

These relationships live beyond obligation. They are rooted in alignment. They remind you what life can feel like when it's not about proving... but simply *being*. This is the joy that arrives when you stop chasing connection and start attracting alignment.

This is the circle that forms when you've made peace with who you are.

You are "home." You can just BE.

These connections bring joy, depth, and a sacred kind of silliness, the kind where inside jokes are born in minutes, and every gathering feels like ceremony and celebration rolled into one.

There's lightness here. There's magic.

This is the reward for doing the hard, spiritual work of choosing yourself.

Reunions with the past may still happen. You may see old friends, and you'll feel the distance. Celebrate the renewed self-respect for how far you've come. It isn't arrogance; it's reverence for the healed version of you.

And sometimes... the old circle won't celebrate your becoming.

Your glow might make others uncomfortable. Your boundaries might be read as rejection. Your healing might reflect back to them the parts they've avoided in themselves.

It can feel confusing, especially if you once shared deep bonds. But remember not everyone is meant to walk every step of the path with you. They are here but for a season.

Some connections fade, not in flames, but in quiet completion. You stop reaching. They stop asking. The texts slow. The invitations pause. Slowly, the cords loosen.

Let them. Let the old circle dissolve with peace and dignity. You can honor what was without dragging it into what *is*.

Because what's ahead of you isn't built on guilt. It's built on truth. Here you breathe deeply and freely.

And those who are meant to meet you in this next chapter? They'll recognize you by your frequency, not your history.

The Thirst for More

When the old shell cracks, you feel the thirst for deeper work. You long for healing that doesn't just soothe the surface but reaches the root. This is where shadow work enters.

For me, shadow work didn't arrive as a concept in a psychology book, it came as the uncomfortable moments when I realized the parts of myself I was most ashamed of or the most afraid of held the very power I needed to reclaim.

The shadow showed itself in the anger I didn't want to admit, in the fears I thought I had buried. It was my own invitation to go deeper.

But here's the truth most people don't talk about: When I first embarked on my healing journey, I wasn't doing shadow work. I was doing *survival healing*, pulling myself out of the sludge-filled basement, reclaiming my worth, learning to function again.

That healing was necessary. Sacred. Life-saving.

It wasn't until much later, as I deepened my relationship with Source, that I began to glimpse just how vast the terrain of the shadow really was. I had thought I'd done the work.

But that work is never entirely done. What felt like having done the work was merely scratching the surface and peeling back another layer in the onion of life.

You see, the shadow doesn't often reveal itself in the first wave of healing. It waits. It knows when you're strong enough to face it without collapsing.

When you've built enough trust with yourself, with Source, with your inner voice...*then* the shadow self steps forward.

Getting into the shadows wasn't something I could have done at the beginning.
I needed the scaffolding of earlier healing to hold me.
I needed self-compassion.
I needed a baseline of safety and spiritual connection. Without that, I would've mistaken my shadows for shame and run from them all over again.

But when I was ready... they came.

And only when I understood the significance of embracing those shadows, rather than avoiding them, did fundamental transformation begin.

This wasn't a surface shift.

This was soul-deep remembering.

Shadow work didn't replace healing. It *expanded* it. It brought me home to parts of myself I never knew I was allowed to love.

I learned to love the part of me that needed rest, the part I had once labeled lazy or weak simply because it refused to keep pushing past its limits. I learned to listen to my anger and resentment, not as something to suppress or be ashamed of, but as messengers pointing me back to my boundaries. I learned that taking up space did not require justification, explanation, or permission. I could simply be present, fully myself, without shrinking or apologizing.

Most of all, I learned to love the intuitive, imaginative, and unconventional parts of me. The spiritual curiosity and creativity I once tried to soften or hide were never flaws. They were the very things that set me free. Shadow work didn't ask me to fit a different role. It gave me permission to stop playing roles altogether.

Shadow Work

The term "shadow work" may sound "woo," but it actually comes from Carl Jung (1875–1961), who described the shadow as the unconscious aspects of ourselves that we suppress or deny.

The shadow isn't only negative; it holds both the qualities we reject *and* the potential we repress. Anger, shame, envy, but also creativity, power, and brilliance that we pushed aside to fit into expectations.

Key truths about the shadow:

The Dark Side and Beyond: It's the hidden side of us, shaped by what we were told was "unacceptable."

Our shadow is formed from all the parts of ourselves we felt we had to hide, anger that wasn't allowed, sadness that made others uncomfortable, desires that were judged, instincts that were shamed. Over time, these pieces get pushed underground, not because they are bad, but because the world around us didn't know how to hold them. The shadow becomes the storage room for everything we weren't permitted to be.

Repressed Potential: Alongside what we dislike may be gifts and talents we've hidden.

The shadow isn't just where we tuck away our wounds, it's where we hide our brilliance too. Many people bury their confidence, ambition, sexuality, intuition, leadership, or creativity because those qualities once threatened their belonging. In reclaiming the shadow, we often find strengths that have been waiting for decades to be acknowledged.

Projection: Often, the traits we judge most harshly in others are mirrors of what we've denied in ourselves.

Projection is one of the clearest ways the shadow reveals itself. When someone else's behavior triggers you more intensely than the situation warrants, that reaction is a clue. We tend to react strongest to traits we've exiled from ourselves. What we can't tolerate in others is often something we haven't made peace with internally.

Shadow work is not about destroying the shadow but integrating it. By welcoming it into awareness, we reclaim wholeness.

How to Explore the Shadow

Notice projections: your strongest emotional reactions are clues.

When a reaction feels outsized or sticky, pause before judging it. Ask yourself what part of this emotion belongs to the present moment, and what part feels older, familiar, patterned, or rooted in something deeper. These reactions are invitations to look inward rather than outward.

Reflect on dreams: messages from the unconscious.
Dreams are one of the safest places the shadow reveals itself. Symbolic, exaggerated, or unusual dreams often point to feelings we haven't fully processed in waking life. Recording and reflecting on them can offer insight into what your deeper self is trying to bring forward.

Use imagination and journaling to explore hidden parts.
Writing, imagery, and guided visualization can help bypass the filters of the conscious mind. These practices allow you to "meet" the shadow as a part of you: the one that has something to say, something to teach, and something to be released.

The Benefits of Integration

Less self-sabotage and inner conflict.
When the shadow runs the show from underground, it often expresses itself through self-defeating choices. Once acknowledged, these behaviors lose their hidden power, and your inner world becomes more cooperative and grounded.

Greater authenticity and creativity.
As suppressed qualities come back online, you stop performing and start expressing. Your creativity returns, your voice sharpens, and your relationships become more honest because you are no longer hiding from yourself.

Access to suppressed gifts and energy.
Integration releases the energy it once took to keep the shadow buried. This often shows up as renewed confidence, clearer boundaries, intuitive clarity, and a surprising sense of vitality.

A sense of maturity, wholeness, and peace.
When you welcome all parts of yourself, you stop fighting internal battles and start living from a grounded center. Wholeness isn't perfection, it's the ability to hold all of you with compassion.

I once worked with a client who came to me feeling stuck in every area of her life. She described herself as indecisive, fearful, and constantly worried about disappointing others.

As we worked together, we uncovered that beneath her 'fear' was actually a fierce independence that had been buried since childhood, shamed as being 'too much' or 'too bossy.' Through shadow work, she learned to reclaim that independence, not as arrogance, but as clarity and confidence.

It didn't happen overnight, but slowly, her decisions became easier. She no longer apologized for her truth. What she once saw as a flaw was actually one of her greatest gifts.

Healing With Support

This is tender work. You can do parts of it alone, but you don't have to. Safety accelerates healing.

Shadow work is not meant to be done alone. Old traumas, blocks, and limiting beliefs rise to the surface in this process. Having a mentor or coach, someone who can hold a safe, energetic container, is essential.

In my work, I gently guide clients through uncovering these patterns, helping them release what no longer serves, and supporting them as they integrate their healed selves. This work is not about breakdowns, but breakthroughs.

From here, the healed self becomes the guide. Each layer of shadow that is integrated brings more freedom, more authenticity, and more power to live as the soul always intended.

Closing Reflection

The shadow is not something to fear. It is the forgotten part of us that longs to come home.

When we stop fighting it and start listening, we discover that even our darkest corners hold light.

The journey of integration is what allows us to live whole, authentic, and free, no longer molded by expectations, but guided by our soul.

Journal Prompt

Take a quiet moment to reflect on the parts of yourself you've been taught to hide or reject.

What qualities or patterns feel "unacceptable" or "too much"?

Write about where they came from, who first told you they were not okay, and consider how those same traits might hold hidden gifts or strengths.

Where am I still performing instead of living? List three places I'm ready to trade approval for alignment, and the first tiny action I'll take this week.

Affirmation: I choose alignment over approval, every time.

____

____

____

____

____

____

____

____

Chapter 6

The Transparency Tension

To be yourself in a world that is constant.
I trying to make you something else
is the greatest accomplishment.
Ralph Waldo Emerson

I used to think there was safety in keeping parts of myself hidden. I didn't lie, I just *didn't say everything.* I can be intuitive without using the word *'psychic.'* I could help people without needing to explain *how* I knew what they needed. I could offer energy work without mentioning Source that moved through it all.

Living in the Midwest, it felt easier to let people fill in the blanks rather than speak the truth myself.

But something shifted. Slowly at first, then all at once. The hiding started to feel heavy.
It wasn't shameful. It was self-protection.

A quiet agreement I made with the world:

"I'll help, but I won't disturb."

Only the truth is: transformation is always a little disruptive. Source doesn't do half-truths.

The Midwestern Mask

Iowa is home. It's land that raised me and still holds me. But it's also a place where practicality often gets more respect than possibility. People want to see what they're buying. They want results they can measure.

Anything too mystical can quickly get labeled as "woo."

Or like my bestie likes to tease, "You know you are selling Magic Beans..." to which I say, "Technically, the magic beans worked! They grew a beanstalk, and that was the thing that brought fortune and abundance to Jack and his family."

It's not said with malice, just that classic Midwestern side-eye that says, "We love you, but also... what are you doing exactly?"

For a long time, I played by those rules. I talked about wellness, mindset, and balance. All good things. All *true*. But incomplete.

Because what do I *really* do?

I hold space for people to remember their wholeness.
I tune in to what's unspoken.
I clear energy that doesn't belong.
I witness healing at the cellular, ancestral, and spiritual levels.

That can't always be quantified, but it can be *felt*.

The more I tried to shapeshift to be palatable, the more fragmented I felt until the cost of staying silent outweighed the risk of being seen.

The Moment I Said It Out Loud

It didn't happen on a stage.
It wasn't a big announcement.
It was in a simple conversation with a longtime family friend, where I finally said, *"I'm a spiritual healer."*

Not a coach.
Not a wellness guide.
Not intuitive support.
But *healer.*

The words vibrated in my throat like something ancient, waiting lifetimes to be spoken. My chest burned, not with fear, but with recognition.

I recall that immediate sense of relief. Thinking "There, I said it!"

At first, the words felt flippant as they fell from my mouth. I felt a pregnant pause. My mind raced to fill the void I anticipated. And the family friend? She didn't flinch. She exhaled. She *knew*.

That's when it hit me: People weren't afraid of what I am. I was scared of what it meant to claim it.

Each time I say it now, "I'm a healer," it gets softer and stronger all at the same time. Solidifying who *I Have Become*. My truth settling into its home.

Another Local Conversation

And yet, there are surprises.

I remember volunteering with a group when the topic of being published came up. One woman mentioned she'd read my book and enjoyed it. Later, she asked what I was up to that day, and I told her I was headed to a metaphysical fair in a neighboring town.

When she pressed for details, I admitted I'd be there as an intuitive healer or psychic, offering mini energy readings. I braced myself for the awkward silence I thought would surely follow.

Instead, she leaned in, literally leaned in, and asked thoughtful questions about the event, my practice, and how this work might support her.

That's the tension of transparency here in the Midwest. Sometimes my declaration of "I'm an intuitive healer" gets met with a raised eyebrow and a polite "Oh..." Other times, it opens doors to deeper conversations.

Either way, every time I speak it out loud, I shed a little more of the mask.

The Dance Between Seen and Safe

Coming out of the spiritual closet isn't a one-time event. It's a series of choices, each one an invitation to be more visible, more whole, more honest. Sometimes it's uncomfortable.

Sometimes I still hesitate when someone asks, "So what do you do?" I feel into who they are, what they're ready to receive, and what I feel appropriate to share.

Not out of fear, but discernment. Transparency isn't about revealing everything to everyone. It's about not hiding the truth from yourself.

It really is a dance. Some days, the music feels safe, and I step forward boldly. Other days, I take smaller steps, protecting my space. Both are part of the choreography of becoming.

Transparency isn't about revealing everything to everyone. It's about not hiding the truth from yourself.

I no longer need to wrap my work in language that dilutes it. I trust that the people who are meant to find me will align with this frequency.

And those who don't? They're not my assignment. Not everyone is my cup of tea, my client, or my anything. I'm okay with learning that.

The Cost of Containment

There's an invisible tax on hiding. Every time you shrink your truth to fit someone else's comfort, you lose a little more of your light.

I used to think I was keeping the peace by staying small. What I was really doing was keeping myself from peace.

It's taken me years to unlearn that kind of self-erasure. To realize that humility and invisibility are not the same thing. You can be humble and still take up space. You can be spiritual and still be seen.

When we talk about authenticity, we often forget that it requires risk. To live your truth, you must be willing to disappoint a few expectations.

That's okay. Because the truth always costs something, but it gives back tenfold in freedom.

A Word to the Ones Still Hiding

If you're someone who knows you have gifts, and you've been afraid to name them, know this:

You're not broken for playing small. You were keeping yourself safe in a world that hasn't always been safe for magic.

If your family or community dismissed your gifts, told you you were crazy, or laughed at your knowing, please understand that was about their fear, not your truth. You are not too much. You were simply tuned in.

Also know: Your truth is medicine, not just for others, but for *you as well.*

There will come a moment when staying hidden will hurt more than being misunderstood. When that moment arrives, let it. Let the truth ring out of you in your own way, in your own time. Whisper it. Shout it. Write it. Pray it. Paint it.

But let it live.

It comes on its own time, like a new baby waiting to be born. Not scheduled, rehearsed, or planned, but when it is right.

Because when we tell the truth about who we are, we give others permission to do the same.

That's leadership.
That's legacy.
That's healing.

The Inner Filter

In my circle, we joke about losing our "inner filter" as we age. But I've come to believe it's not about losing decorum, it's about gaining comfort in your own skin. This is one of my favorite aspects of working with the geriatric population. Losing that filter seems to be a rite of passage.

When you shed the fear of judgment, you stop performing for approval. When you're anchored in authenticity, when your energy comes from pure heart-space, there's nothing to judge.

That's freedom. That's the moment you stop editing yourself for a world that was never meant to understand you completely.

Closing Reflection

Healing isn't a single event; it's a process of returning to yourself again and again.

Every release, every realization, every moment of surrender is another step toward freedom. The journey isn't about becoming someone new; it's about remembering who you've always been; unfiltered.

Journal Prompt

What is one belief, pattern, or old story that you are ready to release? Write it down, then imagine what your life could look like without carrying it.

Chapter 7

✳

The Cycles of Emergence

***The wound is the place where
the Light enters you.***
Rumi

There are seasons when I vanish.

Not physically. Not dramatically. But inwardly. I pull back. I go quiet. I stop marketing, stop offering, stop trying to *be seen*.

For a long time, I made myself wrong for that.

In a world that praises consistency and visibility, disappearing can feel like failure. But I've come to realize, those seasons weren't breakdowns. They were breaths.

They were me stepping out of the noise and back into truth. They were moments of re-rooting, when my soul whispered, "Come home. It's time to refill."

They were me returning to Source for my inner work, refilling my well, and waiting for the next wave of truth to rise.

99

I used to think visibility was proof of purpose. Now I know sometimes invisibility is the initiation.

We Don't Evolve in Straight Lines

If you look at my timeline from the outside, it might seem scattered.

Emergency and office medicine. Crisis intervention social worker. Minister. Psychic reader. Mom. Volunteer. Graphic designer. Wellness coach. Float center owner. ThetaHealing® practitioner, Intuitive Healer.

It reads like a single résumé written for ten different people, each version of me doing her best with what she knew at the time.

A woman who used handwriting to read energy, until she didn't. A healer who launched big, then paused. Then came back again, deeper, clearer, changed.

But that's not chaos. Those are cycles.

Growth isn't a staircase, it's a spiral.

How Handwriting Became a Compass

At first, I felt the feelings, intentions, and messages within written words. I thought that was *why* people wrote, to transfer the energy behind their emotions. Then I learned not everyone reads emotion through handwriting.

Years later, I came back to it intentionally. This time, I had both experience and discernment. I had formal training, but I also had spiritual maturity, and that combination changed everything.

Studying Psychographology gave me structure, but life gave me context. Now, when I look at a signature, I don't just see loops and slants. I feel the story of the person behind them, their pace, hesitation, flair, and fire.

Every letter holds a vibration. Every flourish carries a whisper of soul. To me, handwriting isn't analysis, it's energy in motion.

When I began doing design work, that same sensitivity translated beautifully. I could sense the energy my clients wanted but couldn't articulate. Their colors, fonts, and shapes became extensions of their emotional field. Graphic design was just another form of intuitive translation.

That realization changed how I approached all my work: My creativity isn't separate from my spirituality; it *is* my spirituality.

Why the Hiding Happens

Hiding, for me, hasn't always meant fear. Sometimes it's been integration. Sometimes grief. Sometimes, the need to walk through a personal fire before I can guide anyone else.

There have been times when my energy was too tapped to tune into others. When personal crises hit, illness, grief, or overwhelm, I shut down.

It's not avoidance; it's sacred triage. I knew I needed to tend to myself before tending to anyone else. Energy too raw to share isn't a gift, it's a liability.

Other times, hiding has been about reciprocity. Healing is always an exchange. Yes, sometimes that exchange looks like money. But just as often it's gratitude, respect, a hug, or even simple acknowledgment. When the exchange is absent, when I feel used or unseen, I know the balance has tipped. That's when I pull back.

Other times, yes, it's been protection. Because when you're someone who sees and feels deeply, the world can feel too loud.

Showing up visibly as a spiritual healer, particularly in logic-driven spaces where intuition is viewed with suspicion, can touch deep wounds tied to safety, worth, and misunderstanding.

So I retreat. I reset. Then inevitably I re-emerge, stronger, clearer, softer in all the right places.

Each time, a little more me. Each time I've gone quiet, it's because something new was gestating under the surface.

I used to apologize for it. Now I honor it.

I don't continue to give where there's no return energy flow. That's not spiritual, continuing to give without return is self-sabotage.

The Sacred Rhythm of Showing Up (and Stepping Back)

Here's what I've learned: Emergence is not a one-time event. It's a rhythm.

We bloom, not once, but again and again. Like a perennial, it is dormant between seasons. Coming back each year in full bloom, larger and stronger the following year.

Each dormant phase is not an absence; it's alchemy.
Roots deepen in darkness. Flowers don't apologize for winter. Neither should we.

It's like the phases of the moon, waxing into fullness, waning into rest.
It's like breath, inhaling expansion, exhaling release.
It's like the tide, flowing in, flowing out.

Each emergence is a shedding of a skin, a deeper claiming of truth, a renewed alignment with what we're really here to do.

Yes, people may notice your absence. They may wonder what happened. They may even forget for a while.

But when you return in your full frequency, the ones who are meant for you will feel it instantly.

They don't need convincing. They just recognize you.

Finding Balance in Renewal

When I feel drained or disconnected, I no longer try to push through. Instead, I find my balance. For me, that looks like walking in nature, grounding barefoot in the grass, floating, refueling near water, journaling, or creating something just for fun. No goal. No outcome. Just flow.

That's what reignites my energy, stepping out of "output mode" and letting myself receive. Every healer needs that reset, that moment to remember we are part of the rhythm too.

Rest is not a pause in your purpose. It's part of it.

Integration: The Spiral of Becoming

Each cycle of emergence has taught me something new about surrender. Every time I thought I was starting over, I was actually starting deeper.

Sometimes my evolution felt like burnout, but it was really metamorphosis.   Sometimes my silence felt like avoidance, but it was gestation. The spiral doesn't repeat; it refines. You're never back where you began; you're standing on the same ground, but with a higher view from a deeper perspective.

That's what healing is. Not a straight climb, but a beautiful, messy, sacred spiral of remembering who you are, again and again.

Permission to Be Cyclical

If you're reading this and you've felt the pull to pause, to shift, to go inward, *trust it.* You are not behind. You are not broken. You are not inconsistent.

You are in rhythm with your own becoming.

Our gifts are not meant to be broadcast 24/7. They are sacred. They are seasonal. You have permission to ebb and flow, to show up and to rest, to retreat, and to reemerge.

Find your balance. When your energy feels absent, acknowledge it. Then ask: *What reignites me?* For me, it's retreating to nature, letting water and wind recalibrate me. Sometimes it's floating, allowing my brain to sink into theta and my spirit to stretch out.

You'll find your own. It might be a walk, a song, a journal, or simply silence. Whatever it is, honor it.

Because every cycle of hiding has prepared me for the clarity I now carry. Every re-emergence has brought me closer to who I really am.

This book? This moment? This message?

It's my *latest* emergence.

And I have a feeling… it won't be my last.

Closing Reflection

Cycles of hiding and emerging are part of the spiritual path. At times, we retreat to protect ourselves or to rest. At other times, we step boldly forward to be seen. Neither phase is wrong; both are necessary. The rhythm of expansion and contraction is how we grow into our fullest expression.

Journal Prompt

Think of a time when you felt yourself hiding your gifts or your truth. What were you protecting in that season?

Now reflect on a time when you felt safe to shine. What made that possible?

Part Three:

Living and Leading with Integrity

Chapter 8

The Intuitive Healer's Way

When we heal ourselves, we heal the generations
before us and the generations to come.
Dr. Gabor Maté (paraphrased)

I didn't set out to become a healer.

In fact, for years, I thought what I did was just... something extra.
A sense. A "gift" that was hard to explain. Something I couldn't
quantify or categorize neatly. It was evident in conversations, in
body language, and in the silences between words. While others
seemed to think it was something special, I wasn't always sure
what to do with it.

It wasn't something I trained for; it was something I *remembered.*
The way a musician might suddenly recognize a melody they've
known forever.

People would tell me, "You always know what to say." I'd laugh,
because half the time, I didn't even remember what I'd said; it
just flowed through.

Back then, I didn't call it intuition. I didn't call it psychic ability or energy work. I just called it being me.

Learning Differently

I thought receiving all the energy was "normal." I thought everyone sensed emotions as vividly as I did.

I didn't fully understand that not everyone accesses their gifts. At first, I assumed the difference was simply about being more outspoken. Over time, I realized it went much deeper than that. Not everyone perceives or processes information in the same way.

I learned in college that I truly learn differently from others. I am dyslexic and dysgraphic. My brain processes language, reading and writing differently. At first, that felt like a label, but eventually, it became liberation.

Because while others saw limitations, I saw a design. My wiring made me naturally more intuitive; it tuned me into patterns, energy, and nuance beyond words.

Where others saw data, I felt vibration. Where others memorized, I *remembered by resonance.*

That difference became one of my most excellent tools.

As I enter more like-minded circles where people compare notes, this becomes a genuine difference in how people are made.

In my family, we didn't talk about having gifts. It was accepted to "just know things," so I didn't see it as different. I know now that we are different.

That changed when ThetaHealing® came into my life.

How ThetaHealing® Found Me

When I first encountered ThetaHealing®, I wasn't looking for a modality; I was looking for *relief.*

I had gone through back-to-back life-quakes: a divorce, an identity shift, a career unraveling. Everything I thought I was supposed to be was crumbling.

I found a coach who used ThetaHealing®, and in one of our first sessions, something inside me clicked.

Her process helped me release pain without having to relive it. It felt like being scrubbed clean at a soul level, without reopening old wounds.

I remember the exact moment I knew something had shifted.

I'd spent years saying yes when I meant no, believing it was easier to please than to disappoint. I realized how much of my life had been spent never saying no, just doing, even when it didn't feel right.

That constant "yes" had built up anger in me that, honestly, was justified. Working with my coach, I finally reached deep down, and we pulled out the belief that "saying no makes me selfish."

The forgiveness was real.

When I opened my eyes, I didn't just feel lighter, I felt whole. It was the first time in years I didn't feel like I was waiting for the other shoe to drop.

That was my awakening moment. The anger that had lived in me for decades dissolved, not because someone told me to forgive, but because I finally understood.

Forgiveness wasn't about condoning the past; it was about freeing myself from carrying it.

For the first time, I didn't feel like I had to brace for the next shoe to drop. I looked forward to what came next.

The easiest example is my ex-husband. Before ThetaHealing®, even the thought of him picking up our daughter filled me with dread, sometimes to the point of feeling sick. After the work, the dread was gone.

The facts of the divorce didn't change, but the emotional charge did. That freedom was my biggest "ah-ha," and it's what made me truly embrace the practice.

ThetaHealing® wasn't the first modality I explored. But it was the one that felt like *home.*

Not because it was flashy or filled with rituals, but because it gave language to what I had always done intuitively: drop into a still, connected place... *feel, see, and receive.*

It taught me how to enter the theta brainwave state, connect to Source deliberately and structurally, and witness transformation in real time. It wasn't performance, it was presence. Pure, grounded, and intensely potent.

After that, I knew I didn't want just to receive this kind of healing. I wanted to facilitate it.

Finding My Language

When I began formal training, I was overwhelmed. Every teacher, every modality, every healer seemed to have their own vocabulary. It felt like learning five dialects of the same language, each with its own distinct grammar and tone.

At first, I thought I was doing it wrong. Then I realized, every practitioner has their own glossary. What matters isn't *what you call it*, but *how you connect to it.*

Energy doesn't care about labels. It doesn't need you to call it Reiki, Theta, or intuition. It needs you to honor it, listen to it, and use it responsibly.

That realization changed everything. It took the pressure off performing spirituality and brought me back to *being present.*

What It Means to Be an Intuitive Healer

Now, when people ask what I do, I smile because the answer depends on who's asking and how open they are.

If I'm speaking plainly: I help people clear what no longer serves them, emotionally, energetically, spiritually. I hold sacred space for truth to rise. I tune into patterns, beliefs, and blocks, and with permission, I begin to help shift them, layer by layer. I help people come home to themselves.

ThetaHealing® is the foundation. But over time, I've layered in everything that aligns: Homeopathy, Spiritual coaching, somatic awareness, vibrational insight, and ancestral connection. Each session is different because *each person is different.*

This isn't protocol, it's a partnership. It's not "doing to." It's "being in flow with it."

The Comparison Conversation

Sometimes people ask me: "How is this different from Reiki? From the Emotion Code? From Tarot?"

It's a fair question.

Each of those systems holds value. They all work with energy, just through different doorways. While I deeply respect the integrity of those paths, they are not the tools I was called to develop deeply.

I often explain ThetaHealing® as most like Reiki. The greatest difference? Reiki works to balance and align energies, while ThetaHealing® works to remove the limiting beliefs that *cause* those disruptions, making the results more tangible.

Here's a simple comparison:

I've felt Reiki before. It's gentle and radiant. But I don't channel energy through my hands.

I've explored the Emotion Code and its elegant system of emotional release. But my guidance doesn't follow a chart.

And Tarot, I love the archetypes, the stories, the symbology. But I don't need cards to read what's present.

What I do is tune in:
To your energy
To your words
To your ancestors
To Source
To my Guides
To your Guides
To your Higher Power.
To the field of possibility that exists when we agree: *Something here is ready to shift.*

When I tune into your energy, I send a tendril of my own energy into your field, sensing how it moves and where it settles. I listen for the flow: whether it feels like a one-way street with everything rushing inward or outward, whether it is balanced, warm, inviting, stagnant, or blocked. I experience this as if I am a flowmeter, reading the subtle currents and the spaces between them.

During an energetic scan, I focus on the field around each of the seven primary chakras. I'm looking for areas where energy gathers, slows, or struggles to move. Blockages aren't just "stuck spots;" they often hold stories, beliefs, or experiences that are asking for attention.

When I tune into your words, I feel the weight, cadence, and emotion behind them. I also listen for what is unsaid. This is a form of empathic listening that began during my time as an EMT and deepened during my social work training. Often, the order in which someone describes their pain, or the words they avoid, reveals as much as the words they choose. Over the years, this skill has become one of my most trusted tools in understanding the deeper layers of someone's experience.

While we work together, I may also become aware of your ancestors as they present themselves. They don't always participate, but their presence is often unmistakable, a shift in the air, a sensation just to the side of you, a sense that if I reached out, I could shake their hand. I observe how they respond as you speak, their posture, their interest, and how your body reacts to their presence. All of it becomes part of the larger conversation.

I also listen for messages from Source. Information arrives from many planes and layers, but what comes from Source carries a distinct clarity, resonance, and weight. It feels pure, direct, and steady, like truth crystallized into sound.

I tune into my Guides as well. I work with several, though I don't typically call on archangels or specific beings by name. The Guides who show up are the ones who hold the insight needed in the moment, and they often help clarify or interpret messages from your Guides.

When I call on your Guides, with your permission, it is often at my Guides' prompting. Some Guides come forward simply to witness. They don't always offer information immediately, but when asked, they provide what is needed for the highest good.

I also attune to your Higher Power, whatever that may be within your belief system. These insights often come directly to *you*, not to me. Part of my role is helping you recognize and interpret the messages you're receiving in real time.

All of this describes the general landscape of how I work. When there are specific concerns or requests during a scan, reading, or healing session, we address those intentionally. There are times when I encounter limited access to someone's energy. When that happens, we pause and revisit the foundational question of permission, what you're truly seeking, what you feel ready for, and where your boundaries need honoring. The work continues, but it continues with integrity.

I don't predict the future. I don't diagnose. I don't heal you.

I *witness* your healing. That's the distinction, and it's sacred.

When to Speak and When to Listen

My role is to help individuals define their own goals and empower them with the tools to get there. When I help them see the brilliance in themselves, they become unstoppable.

Healing isn't about superiority; it's about partnership. I don't stand above my clients; I stand beside them. When I hold space, it's not from authority, it's from awe.

There's a sacred balance in knowing when to speak and when to stay silent. Sometimes Source floods me with information, but the real wisdom is in restraint. Because truth without timing can wound, and a healer without humility can harm.

Lessons in Discernment

There was a time I was scheduled for a reading. Something felt off from the beginning. My system kept sending me signals: my booking platform glitched, the video wouldn't connect, and I lost track of time.

Every sign screamed, "Not today." But I ignored them. I didn't want to disappoint anyone.

That session was chaos. Nothing landed, the energy was heavy, and I felt completely off my axis. It took me weeks and a few good mentoring sessions to recover my equilibrium. I learned in that opportunity, not to extend my energy when it is not in alignment.

Now, I listen. When resistance builds like a wall, it's not always a test; it's often a sign. Sometimes, the bravest act is to reschedule and honor that knowing. Sometimes best NOT to engage at all.

Following the path of least resistance isn't laziness; it's alignment.

Energy Is an Exchange

Healing is always a two-way flow. When energy exchange is balanced, both people leave nourished. When it's not, someone leaves drained.

Money, gratitude, kindness, or reciprocity, they all count. It's not the *form* of the exchange that matters, but the *integrity* of it.

I've learned that the body is a perfect barometer. If I walk away from a session feeling heavy or foggy, it's a sign that something was off. If I feel bright, clear, and grounded, I know we were both in the right energetic exchange.

The Power of Permission

Everything I do begins with consent. Not just the spoken "yes," but the energetic readiness of the soul.

I never enter someone's energy field without asking. Even if they're a paying client.

Permission is not a formality; it's a sacred contract. It's saying, "I honor your autonomy. I walk beside you, not within you."

That's why I always ask before shifting beliefs. Before clearing pain. Before rewriting stories.

Healing isn't something I *do to* someone. It's something I *walk through with* them.

For me, to "fix" someone would be to disempower them. First, no one is broken. Second, I see my role as guiding and holding space so an individual can define their own goals and move toward their highest good. My role is to provide skills and tools, and to mirror back the awesomeness I see in them. When someone has even one person who truly believes in them, they become unstoppable.

I see myself as a lighthouse, not a lifeguard. I shine a beam of light so people can find their way. I don't drag them to shore.

Becoming Your Own Healer

One of the most powerful realizations in my journey is this: Everyone is intuitive. Everyone has access to healing.

Some of us have simply remembered sooner. We have just walked farther down the path and are now turning to light the pathway for others.

So, no, my role isn't to be special. *It's to be true.* To live what I teach. To show up in my fullness, grounded in what works for me, and serve from overflow.

That's the way of the intuitive healer.

An intuitive healer isn't the one who knows everything; it's the one who listens deeply. Who hears what's said and unsaid. Who trusts that the silence between words can be just as healing as any technique.

The one who holds space for the truth to rise.

When you hold space from that place of authenticity, miracles don't just happen, they unfold naturally.

Closing Reflection

There are many paths to connection: Tarot, Reiki, Emotion Code, ThetaHealing®. None is "better" or "worse." They are simply doorways. What matters is not the tool, but the alignment between the healer, the seeker, and Source. When you trust your way of connecting, you step fully into your power as an intuitive being.

Journal Prompt

What tools or practices help you feel most connected to your intuition or Source? How do you know when something is in alignment for you, and when it's not? Do you feel it in your physical being? If so, where?

____

____

____

____

____

____

____

____

Chapter 9

The Ethics of Reading Energy

With great power comes great responsibility.
Voltaire (or Spider-Man's Uncle Ben)

Discernment is not judgment.
It is clarity with compassion.
Amanda Beth Johnson

The Weight of Receiving Information

If I can see something, sense something, or hear something, does that mean I should say it?

That's the question I ask myself every single time I receive information.

Because information flows constantly. Sometimes it's a whisper. Sometimes it's a blunt, undeniable flash. My responsibility as a healer is not just to *receive* it, but to discern:

Was this meant for me?

Was this meant for someone else?

And if it *was* meant for them, am I meant to deliver it now, or not at all?

In my early days, I often struggled to refrain from blurting things out. It felt impulsive, almost like what those with attention challenges describe, filtering through the flood to find what's actually essential. Over time, I learned to pause, to sort, to respect the weight of the message.

Sometimes the message is for me, and I've learned to file it away in my "past, present, or future" drawers. Sometimes it makes no sense until months later. Sometimes, it's for the person in front of me, but even then, timing and delivery matter.

Permission Is Sacred

Whether I am seeking information for myself or for someone else, permission is everything.

For myself, mornings are my most sacred time. Before I touch my phone, turn on the TV, or consume anything external, I sit in silence with my coffee. This is when I can truly hear.

Sometimes I speak to Source. Sometimes I seek wisdom from my future self. Sometimes I listen to the whispers of my inner child.

Each "voice" has its own way of communicating, much like teachers in school who each required a different approach. Some were encouraging, some direct, some patient, some challenging. The key was never whether the teacher existed, but whether you understood how to listen, what they were asking of you, and why.

Not every inner voice carries the same authority. Part of discernment is learning to recognize the difference between your own thoughts, the influence of fear or ego, the guidance of spiritual helpers, and information that comes from Source itself. This distinction matters. Source communicates without agenda. The message is clear, neutral, and supportive of your highest good. It does not rush, threaten, or flatter. It does not ask you to abandon your sovereignty .

Guides and Angels, while supportive, are still individual consciousnesses. Their messages can carry personality. They may feel playful, encouraging, or even gently humorous. Over time, you may notice differences in tone. For me, messages that feel lighthearted, joking, or conversational often come from Guides, while messages from Source feel grounded, precise, and deeply steady.

Discernment also requires looking at the intention behind the message. What is it asking you to do? Does it expand your sense of choice or narrow it? Does it invite clarity, responsibility, and growth, or does it lean on urgency, fear, or dependency? Sometimes the most important part of discernment is not the message itself, but whether the question being asked was clear and intentional.

This kind of discernment is not immediate. It develops with practice, reflection, and self-awareness. Over time, you begin to trust how information feels in your body. You learn the difference between imagination, intuition, and true guidance. Permission is sacred not because messages are rare, but because listening wisely is a skill that deepens with care.

With clients, permission becomes even more crucial. Before I ever enter someone's energetic space or connect with their Guides, I ask. Even if they look at me like, *Of course you can, I'm paying you!* I still ask. It's part of honoring the sacredness of the process.

In the early days, when I worked with handwriting, I would ask people to sign their name and write a short sentence on an unlined index card. Yes, the energy was in the ink, but unless they gave explicit permission, it wasn't mine to read. Without that consent, it felt like peeking through someone's window. Just because energy is present doesn't mean it's free for me to access.

Permission is like knocking on a door before you enter. It creates a sense of safety, respect, and openness for both the client and me.

Guides, Gatekeepers, and Boundaries

Meeting with someone's Guides is like being invited to a social gathering. Each has its own personality. Some are humorous. Some are blunt. Some are ancestors. All of them, while wise, are not the same as Source.

As a ThetaHealing® practitioner, I connect to Source first, then return to meet with Guides, my own or those of my clients. My own Guides often show up as a "board of directors." Not every member attends every meeting; those who do are the ones relevant to the work at hand. Some I know by name, others by their presence, a scent, or a unique feeling.

When I meet with a client's Guides, they usually confirm what I've already perceived in my energetic scan, adding reminders, affirmations, or additional details. Sometimes they sigh in exasperation, like, *"We've been trying to tell them this forever!"* Sometimes they present new symbology I've never encountered before.

This is where I often ask my clients: *Does this make sense?* It's not about fishing for validation. It's about ensuring I translate the new symbol in a way that resonates with them. If I see a rocking horse, I don't assume its meaning; I ask what it means to them.

From there, I can understand the symbol as it applies to their life story and offer truly personal guidance.

When I first began this work, I called myself a reader. That word felt safe. People understood it, whether I was reading handwriting, energy, or the emotions tucked between someone's words. A reader observes and reflects back on what is seen.

But as my practice deepened, I realized my role was never just about giving information. The messages were only the doorway. What mattered was how people used those insights to change their lives, to release, to heal, to grow. That was when I understood: I am not only a reader. I am a healer. My role is not to predict or to entertain, but to hold space where transformation becomes possible.

Boundaries are just as important as permission. Clients who have experienced trauma often have built tall, protective walls. Part of my role is creating a safe environment so they can lower those walls voluntarily. *Without that trust, no healing can happen.*

What to Share and What Not to Share

Being a healer means becoming the "mom of the information." I hold it carefully, with discernment, asking:

How will this serve the person?
Is this part of their puzzle right now?
Will this build their bridge, or overwhelm them?

Sometimes clients don't understand what I've shared until weeks or months later. And that's okay. When it finally clicks, it often lands more gently.

Some of the most challenging pieces of information I've received were about past lives. When I read for someone, I often *feel* what they experienced. Once, I read for a profoundly gifted individual who was paralyzed by the fear of stepping into their power. I could feel their past-life trauma as if it were my own: the stones, the pain, the terror of persecution. It was uncomfortable, but by delivering it gently, I helped them recognize the root of their fear and release it.

This was an instance in which consulting their Guides proved invaluable. Through that exchange, I could tell whether the insight was something entirely new or simply affirming a feeling they already carried. Their Guides also helped me understand the most supportive way to offer the message, its tone, its timing, and the manner in which it would be most gently received.

That's the discernment. Not everything should be spoken bluntly, even if it arrives at me bluntly. My responsibility is to translate it in a way the person can process, integrate, and use.

When It Gets Personal

Ethics aren't just for clients. They've been forged in my own fire.

At metaphysical fairs, when there were lulls, we often traded readings to keep energy moving. I discovered an intense aversion to amber, so strong it made me violently ill. Other readers suggested it was tied to a past life. Sure enough, in regressions (both guided and spontaneous, like during floats), I uncovered memories of being run over by wagon wheels, struggling to breathe, and other traumas that lingered in my body's memory.

The most intense experience occurred during a spiritual retreat following a kundalini awakening. In a chanting circle, surrounded by people I trusted, I suddenly felt unsafe and attacked. My instinct was to shield, but I was told, *"This isn't about them." This is about you.* You can't shield against yourself.

The pain surged in my feet and legs. My hands felt bound. I looked down and saw myself being burned at the stake.

The terror was absolute, but so was the release. By acknowledging it, I could finally let it go. That memory, too, no longer defines me.

These experiences are why I take my work so seriously, why I hold boundaries, and why I respect timing because I know the weight of information that arrives unbidden, and how powerful it can be when handled with care.

My past-life memories have varied in intensity, and not all of them have been negative. When they arrive with deep emotional force, they require time, support, and careful guidance to process. Having walked through that myself, I carry an added layer of concern when such information arises for a client. Are they in a place where they can receive it? Do they have the support they need to integrate it? Most often, clients have already sensed these truths on some level, and I am simply helping to confirm and release the emotional states or limiting beliefs connected to them.

The Healer's Responsibility

Having intuition, being a reader, and accessing someone else's energy without their consent is invasive. It's wrong. And it's exhausting.

With permission, the work flows through Source and leaves me whole. Without it, it drains me.

That's why I honor timing. Some clients require icebreakers and small talk before they feel comfortable opening up. Some individuals require more extended sessions, as 15 minutes may not provide sufficient closure. I've often found myself helping someone process an incomplete reading from another practitioner at live events before I can even begin my work with them.

A reading or healing must always end with a sense of completion. I often ask, *"Do you feel complete?" Did we finish what you came for today?*

Because I believe the healer's responsibility isn't just to share what we see, it's to ensure safety, integrity, and closure.

Sometimes the most ethical choice is to keep the information quiet. Just because you hear something in the grocery line doesn't mean you repeat it. Gossip is low vibrational energy. The same is true in Spiritual work: discernment is everything.

Have your code of ethics. And follow it.

Closing Reflection

Intuition without ethics is intrusion.

It is not enough to see, hear, or feel; you must also discern when and how to share. Permission, timing, and compassion are what transform raw perception into healing guidance.

Holding information with respect, honoring boundaries, and allowing space for closure are what make the difference between wounding and healing. True integrity as a healer isn't about what you can access; it's about what you choose to honor.

Journal Prompt

Reflect on a time when you knew something about another person, whether through intuition, observation, or "just a feeling." How did you handle it?

Looking back, would you choose to share it, soften it, or keep it to yourself? What does this teach you about your own personal code of ethics?

____

____

____

____

____

____

____

____

Chapter 10

Labels and Boxes

***You were never meant to shrink to fit into
someone else's version of acceptable.
You were born to expand.***
Lalah Delia

We invest so much time trying to label things, to categorize, define, and keep everything neatly contained.

We do it with people, with beliefs, and even with our pain. It feels safer when we can put something in a box and slide it onto a mental shelf marked "Known."

But I've never been very good at that. I don't like boxes. I don't like walls. And I especially don't like coloring inside lines that someone else drew.

Recently, during a client session, this came up again, one of those full-circle lessons Source likes to deliver when you least expect it.

She was struggling to balance the multiple roles in her life: mother, caregiver, business owner, empath, people-pleaser, and perfectionist. Each label had its own set of invisible rules, and she was exhausted trying to live up to them all.

As we worked through it, she blurted out, "But who am I if I'm not all of those things?" That question landed in my chest like a bell ringing in a cathedral.

We are born whole, fluid, connected to everything, and then the world starts sticking labels on us like price tags. Some we take willingly; others get stamped on us before we ever have a say.

I looked at her and said, "Maybe you're not supposed to be *just one thing.* Maybe your work isn't to find the perfect label, but to outgrow the ones that no longer fit."

Even as I said it, I could feel Source smiling because that's been one of my lifelong lessons, too.

My Lifelong Battle with Boxes

I've never liked being boxed in, figuratively or literally.

Back in my print advertising days, I had one non-negotiable rule: *no boxes around my ads.* Everyone else loved borders and outlines, saying it made the content look "clean." I hated it. The box always felt like it trapped the message's energy, keeping it from breathing.

Now, looking back, I realize that was more than a design preference. It was a reflection of how I move through life. Even then, I didn't want my message contained.

That same resistance shows up in my spiritual work. Every class I've taken, every certification I've pursued, seems to begin with the question, "So, what kind of practitioner are you?"

It's meant as an icebreaker, but it always lands like a limitation.

The Quiz That Started It

Not long ago, another practitioner, bright, earnest, new to her gifts, looked at me and asked, "So... what kind of witch am I?"

In my mind's eye, I instantly saw one of those *Seventeen Magazine* quizzes: *Pick a crystal, choose your favorite moon phase, tally your points, and voilà, you're a kitchen witch!*

It made me laugh, but it also made me a little sad. The need to categorize ourselves stems from the same conditioning that tells us we need permission to exist.

We are infinite beings with infinite ways to express who we are. But when we start slapping labels on everything, we start trimming away the edges of our truth. We go from *becoming* to *belonging*, and not always in a healthy way.

I told her, "You're the kind of witch who's still unfolding. That's the best kind there is."

She smiled, and I could feel her energy soften. That's when it clicked for both of us: labels might give temporary comfort, but they also create cages.

Learning Inside the Lines (and Outside Them)

As I've formalized my spiritual practice, taken more classes, and earned certifications, I've often felt like an outsider peeking through the window.

There are so many names for things, mediumship, channeling, light language, clair-this and clair-that, that sometimes the actual work gets lost in the definitions.

I can remember sitting in workshops, pen in hand, watching everyone else nod like they already knew the language. I was still figuring out which glossary we were using.

It took me a long time to realize that every teacher, every modality, and every lineage has its own vocabulary. It's like traveling to new countries: same essence, different dialects.

At first, I felt utterly lost. I thought I must be doing something wrong if I couldn't explain exactly *how* I knew what I knew.

But the truth is, I didn't need to name it. I just needed to trust it.

The Client, the Booth, and the Corner Box

Then there are the literal boxes, the kind made of booth poles and drapes at metaphysical fairs.

Recently, I was assigned a booth space that, let's say, was less than ideal. An inverted corner. The least desirable spot. It meant people could approach only from one direction, at a narrow angle. My inner designer and my inner empath both cringed.

I sat there, staring at my little box, wondering if the universe was laughing. Then it hit me, of course, I was in the corner. Of course, I was boxed in. Because I still had more to learn about what it means to make space, not just take-up space.

As I started setting up my table, I felt that familiar overthinking kick in: What's the traffic flow? Will people even see me? Should I move my books closer to the aisle?

Like a whisper, I heard, *Stop worrying about the box. Focus on the energy inside it.*

So, I did. I grounded. I breathed. I let Source fill the space, even if the layout didn't make sense to my logical left brain.

Wouldn't you know, it turned into one of the busiest, most connected events I've had in years.

When Labels Collide

Another day, I was talking with a nurse coach, a logical, clinical mind who was exploring homeopathy outside the clinical setting. We discussed another practitioner who described herself as both a nurse coach *and* a heart healer on her website.

She frowned and said, "I'm okay with psychic or intuitive, but *medium?* That's a step too far."

Her reaction sat with me for weeks. I wasn't offended; I was just fascinated. The word *medium* had tripped something in her.

It reminded me of the power of words and the baggage specific labels carry. Say you're "psychic," and people picture a crystal ball. Say "medium," and they imagine a seance. Say "intuitive," and they nod politely.

For a while, I let that awareness silence me. I stopped using the word 'medium' to describe any of the work I did. I chose the "softer" labels: coach, reader, and intuitive healer, because they caused less friction. But deep down, I knew I was dimming my truth to make others comfortable.

But later, on a podcast, the host casually referred to mediumship as "another way intuition speaks." He said it so matter-of-factly that it made me laugh.

All that tiptoeing I'd done around language, and here was someone saying it like it was the most normal thing in the world.

That's when I realized, the fear was mine. The labels weren't the problem. The judgment I attached to them was.

Now, when I introduce myself, I let the word "healer" land fully. Sometimes it gets a raised eyebrow. Sometimes it opens a door. But either way, it's *true.*

And truth, I've learned, is the only label that fits.

Fluidity Over Form

The deeper I go into this work, the more I realize that intuition itself is fluid. Some days, I'm deeply clairvoyant, seeing crisp, vivid images. Other days, I'm mostly clairsentient, feeling waves of emotion through my own body.

Sometimes messages come as smells or tastes. Once, while doing energy work for a client, I suddenly smelled cigarette smoke. Neither of us smoked. Later, she told me her grandfather, whom she'd been thinking of all weeks, was a lifelong smoker.

Those moments remind me: it's not about mastering *all* the senses. It's about staying open.

When we demand that our intuition behave consistently, we start boxing it in again.

Source doesn't do repetition; it does alignment.

So let your gifts show up however they want to. Don't force them into a single channel just because that's what someone's manual says.

The Boxes We Build for Ourselves

Sometimes the labels don't come from others; they come from us. We say things like, "I'm just empathic," or "I'm only intuitive when it comes to other people," or "I'm not as psychic as so-and-so."

That's us building our own boxes. Or cages.

Every time we compare, we reinforce the idea that there's a hierarchy of gifts. There isn't. There's only alignment and practice.

Some of us are painters, some are poets, and some are both, but we don't tell artists they have to pick one medium. Why do we do that with intuition?

Fluid, Not Fuzzy

Now, fluid doesn't mean flaky. It doesn't mean we drift around aimlessly, changing our label every full moon.

It means we stay responsive, open to evolution, willing to learn, ready to be surprised by what Source reveals next.

Structure has its place; it gives safety. But too much structure becomes a cage. Too much "definition" causes the energy to stagnate.

So yes, I honor the lineages I've studied, ThetaHealing®, homeopathy, somatic awareness, and ancestral clearing, but I refuse to confine myself to one.

Because Source doesn't specialize, it flows.

The Many "Clairs"

People often ask me which of the "clairs" I use most. I usually smile and say, "Whichever one answers the call."

The psychic senses are called the "clairs" from the French word for *clear.* They correspond to our physical senses and sometimes expand beyond them.

Clairvoyance (clear seeing)

Clairvoyance appears to me as images, colors, or symbols that appear in my inner vision. I often get images/symbols of keys and locks, animals, or rocks. They usually come in the final moments of a session, like the energetic period at the end of a sentence. I may suddenly see a key sliding into a lock, a rainbow stretching across a quiet sky, or the ocean lapping softly at the shore. These visions aren't random. When the picture arrives, it tells me the reading has come full circle, that all the pieces have settled into place. For instance, at the end of one session, I saw a small, weathered key resting in a palm. The client had been searching for clarity in a situation where she felt powerless. That simple image told both of us what the energy had been building toward: she already held the key.

Clairaudience (clear hearing)

Clairaudience often arrives as bits of sound, rarely as dramatic, booming voices, but as subtle, meaningful fragments. Sometimes it's a single word, whispered. Other times, it shows up as a few lyrics from a song I haven't heard in years. Once, during a session, I suddenly heard the line *"you're stronger than you know"* from a song I couldn't have recalled on my own. It matched exactly what the client had been wrestling with. I occasionally hear environmental sounds too, a distant train, the clink of dishes, footsteps on gravel, clues pointing to where a memory or message is situated. Clairaudience rarely arrives as a complete sentence; instead, it's a breadcrumb that leads to truth.

Clairsentience (clear feeling)

Clairsentience is one of my strongest gifts. I often feel sensations in my body that mirror what someone else is experiencing, such as physical discomfort, heaviness, or emotional pressure. When someone has a lingering injury, my body will highlight the exact area, sometimes before they even mention it. During one reading, I felt a sharp pull across my right shoulder blade. Moments later, the client confirmed that was where she had been holding pain for months. It's not about absorbing the pain; it's the body's way of saying, *"Here. Start here."* Emotional clairsentience works the same way; I can feel grief settle like a low cloud or joy brighten a room before a single word is spoken.

Clairalience (clear smelling)

Clairalience manifests through scents with no physical source. For me, the smell of cigarettes, specifically the old smell of an ashtray, signals a powerful presence of individuals from my past. These scents appear when I'm facing a challenge, almost like the Universe sending reinforcements. It's as if that familiar aroma carries the message, *"I'm here. Keep going."*

I also receive perfume or cologne scents during readings, often signaling which ancestor or loved one has stepped forward for the client. Sometimes it is sandalwood, sometimes a floral perfume from decades long gone. Though food scents are rarer for me, they do appear occasionally, especially if food was tied to a person's identity or memory. Clairalience is often subtle, yet unmistakably personal.

Clairgustance (clear tasting)

Clairgustance is not as frequent for me, but when it happens, it's distinct. More often than tasting a specific flavor, I experience the *sensation* of taste, like the way sour makes your mouth tighten or how sweetness softens the palate. Once, during a reading, I suddenly felt that sharp, citrus-like tang without any actual flavor. It pointed to an event tied to something "bittersweet" in the client's life, an emotion she had never put into words but instantly recognized. On rare occasions, I've tasted something exact, like chocolate or mint, connected to a person's memory. This gift tends to work more through the body's response than the taste itself.

Claircognizance (clear knowing)

Claircognizance is one of my strongest and most consistent abilities. It's an immediate, unquestioned knowing that has no logical explanation. When I worked in medical settings, I often knew what a patient's lab results or radiology findings would be before the reports ever came back. I couldn't explain how I knew; I just did. And I was usually right. In readings, claircognizance arrives as a sudden clarity, an answer, an insight, or a truth that drops into awareness fully formed. There's no analysis, no debate. It simply *is.* Claircognizance is like the moment when fog lifts, and the entire landscape becomes visible at once.

Clairempathy (clear emotion)

Clairempathy allows me to feel others' emotions directly, not just observe them. This isn't the same as sensing the collective energy of a room. It's more intimate and precise. I can feel someone's sadness settle like a cool weight in the chest, or their fear tighten in the solar plexus. Likewise, joy radiates through me as a lightness, and love feels warm and expansive. In one session, before the client spoke, I felt a wave of quiet grief that didn't belong to me. When she began to share, her words matched exactly what I had already felt. This gift helps me understand not just *what* someone feels, but *how deeply* they are feeling it.

Clairtangency (clear touching)

Clairtangency, or psychometry, comes through physical contact with an object. Some items hold the energy of the people who used, created, or cherished them. Once, at a flea market, I placed my hand on an old sewing machine. Immediately, I felt the presence of the woman who had used it, her rhythm, her patience, her pride in her craft. It was as if her memories had settled into the metal and waited for someone who could feel them. I experience this with jewelry, heirlooms, tools, and even papers. Objects become storytellers; they hold the energetic fingerprints of the lives they've touched. I receive similar vibrations from rocks, but not all of them agree with my sense of vibration.

You don't need to use all of them. You just need to know how *you* receive. The labels are simply descriptions; they're not requirements.

Energy Without Borders

I sometimes think about energy like art supplies. There are watercolor, acrylic, oil, pencil, collage, and all can create something beautiful. But what happens if we mix them? What if we let watercolor spill onto the sketch?

That's what intuition feels like to me. Messy. Alive. Unboxed.

And that's what I want for my clients, to stop worrying about whether they "fit" a label and start exploring what their gifts *feel like* when they're fully expressed.

Because when you stop trying to name it, you start to embody it.

Trusting the Way Your Intuition Arrives

One of the most rewarding parts of my role is helping clients discover how *they* naturally perceive intuitive information. Everyone has access to these abilities, but not everyone receives insight in the same way. Some people see images. Some feel sensations. Some simply "know." And some have spent so many years doubting themselves that their gifts stay tucked beneath layers of self-judgment.

I once worked with a client who had enormous intuitive capacity, although they didn't realize it at first. Whenever I took them through a guided meditation and used phrases like "see," "imagine," or "visualize," they would immediately shut down. The moment they couldn't conjure a picture in their mind; they became frustrated and self-critical. They assumed they were doing it wrong, or worse, that they weren't intuitive at all.

Thankfully, this client trusted me enough to be honest. Instead of pretending to follow along, they said, "I can't do this." That truthfulness opened the door to exactly what they needed.

Over several sessions, we explored how *they* actually perceived information from their Higher Power. We reframed "seeing" not as creating a vivid mental image, but as allowing an idea, sensation, or awareness to rise. When your eyes are closed, darkness is expected, but intuition does not rely on eyesight. It moves through the subtler senses. It reveals itself in impressions, feelings, or subtle shifts that don't look like anything at all.

Once this client let go of the expectation of literal vision, everything changed.

They began to perceive energy in ways that made sense for *them*. They could suddenly identify spaces in their life that needed clearing, physical spaces, emotional spaces, relational spaces. They discovered intuitive abilities they never knew they had and learned to call on specific energies to support their own integration and healing.

This is the kind of work that fills me with awe: guiding someone back to the truth that they are not disconnected from their inner wisdom; they simply haven't yet learned its language.

When clients understand how their intuition speaks to them, something powerful happens. They stop outsourcing their knowing. They stop doubting themselves. They begin participating actively in their healing. They learn to call upon their gifts with purpose and clarity.

The client I mentioned continues to grow in ways neither of us could have predicted during that first session. Their progress has been tremendous, not because I "showed" them anything, but because they discovered how to receive it for themselves. My role was simply to help them get out of their own way.

This is the heart of intuitive development: Not perfection. Not comparison. Not performing spirituality "correctly."

But learning the unique way your inner being speaks and trusting it enough to listen.

Closing Reflection

Labels give us language, but they also give us limits.

Fluidity asks for trust. It asks us to show up without needing to define what will happen next.

You are not one label, one box, one title. You are a living, breathing, expanding soul who learns, forgets, and learns again.

Your work isn't to find the perfect definition; it's to live beyond them.

When you stop asking, "What kind of healer am I?" and start asking, "What truth wants to move through me today?", that's when you step into power.

Journal Prompt

Write down labels you've been given, spiritual, personal, or professional. Which ones feel light and true? Which ones feel heavy or outdated?

Now, imagine placing all those labels in a box. Close the lid. Walk it to a river. Set it in the water and watch it drift away.

Then write the one word that still feels right in your chest.

Let that word be your compass, not your cage.

Afterword

Stepping Into Power

***The privilege of a lifetime is to
become who you truly are.***
Carl Jung

You made it here, through the stories, the lessons, the quiet awakenings. Take a breath and really let that in.

You've walked beside me through my shadows and your own. You've read about courage and discernment, about fear and forgiveness. And now, you stand at the edge of something entirely new: *Your next emergence.*

This isn't the end of the journey. It's the beginning of living it. Because stepping into your power isn't a one-time declaration, it's a practice. It's the way you choose to respond when life tests the truth you've claimed. It's how you soften when your old patterns whisper, "Play small." It's how you remind yourself, again and again: *I am safe to be seen.*

There will still be days you question your light. There will still be moments when the world feels too loud, and your intuition feels like a whisper under the noise. That's okay. Those are invitations to return, not regress. When you forget who you are, come back to presence.

Place your hand on your heart and ask: "What part of me is asking to be witnessed right now?" Then listen. That's where your next step always begins. You don't need another credential to be worthy. You don't need a title, a label, or a box to prove your belonging. You don't have to justify your gifts or defend your sensitivity.

Your authenticity is your authority. Remember that power and tenderness are not opposites; they're dance partners. When you embody both, you become magnetic.

Your energy shifts rooms without you even trying, not because you're louder, but because you're real.

As you close these pages, I want you to know this:
You are not behind.
You are not broken.
You are not late to your purpose.

Everything you have lived, every loss, every ache, every whispered nudge from the universe, has brought you here, perfectly on time.

Keep listening.
Keep grounding.
Keep daring to step into your power, where structure softens, and truth breathes freely.

If this book has done anything, I hope it's reminded you that your light is not meant to be managed, it's meant to be shared. Not in a way that depletes you, but in a way that nourishes everyone it touches, including you.

The work continues every time you choose to lead with love instead of fear. Every time you set a boundary with grace. Every time you speak the truth that trembles on your lips.

That's what it means to live as an intuitive. Not to fix, but to witness. Not to command, but to collaborate.
Not to rise above others, but to rise *with* them.

So here's to you, the courageous soul who keeps showing up, who keeps asking more profound questions, who keeps returning to the well of your own knowing.

May your days be filled with grounded magic.

May your nights bring rest that restores, not hides.

And may you always remember: *You are the healer, the light, the lighthouse, and the sea.*

The work has only just begun, and it starts again and again with you.

The Journey Beyond These Pages

If this book has opened something inside you, a memory, a longing, a spark of recognition, I want you to know there is a path forward that you don't have to walk alone.

Many clients begin their journey with my **Signature Energetic Blueprint**, a compassionate, intuitive reading that reveals your energetic patterns and highlights the places where your healing and growth are ready to unfold. It's a gentle first step that helps you understand where you are, where you're headed, and what your soul is truly asking for.

From there, your journey continues in the way that best supports you. Some move into intuitive healing sessions to release old beliefs and emotional residue. Others step into personal growth or spiritual awakening coaching. Some begin with the deep neurological rest of floatation therapy or the grounding warmth of the BioMat. Every offering is designed to meet you where you are, with safety, curiosity, and respect for your pace.

If you feel called to explore what this next chapter might look like, you are invited to visit:
www.AmandaBethHealing.com.

You can learn more about sessions, book a discovery or clarity call, or simply browse and see what resonates. Additional links and resources are always available at: **www.AmandaBethHealing.com/linktree**.

Take what speaks to you. Leave what doesn't.

This is your journey. I am simply here when you are ready.

Your healing doesn't end when this book does.

It simply begins a new conversation; one you're now ready to have.

A Companion to This Work

In the months ahead, I will also be offering a reflection guide created to walk alongside this book. It is designed for those who want to slow down, reflect, and gently integrate what has stirred within these pages. This is not about doing the work "right," but about giving yourself space to notice, question, and embody what you are remembering.

Alongside the reflection guide, there will be an optional private community where readers can share insights, ask questions, and connect with others moving through this process. Participation is always by choice. Some people learn best in community. Others prefer quiet reflection. Both are honored here.

If you feel drawn to continue this conversation in a more supported way, information about the reflection guide and community will be shared through my website. You are welcome to join when and if it feels right.

http://www.AmandaBethHealing.com/steppingintopower

Meet the Author

Amanda Beth is an intuitive healer, teacher, and writer who believes that authenticity is the highest form of alignment. After decades spent in service roles as a social worker, EMT, business owner, wife, and mother, Amanda Beth found herself burned out, boxed in, and spiritually disconnected. Her awakening led her to study ThetaHealing®, energy medicine, and intuitive ethics, transforming her life and inspiring the work she shares today.

Through private sessions, workshops, and writing, Amanda Beth helps clients step into their power, integrate their healing, and live free from the stories that once defined them. Known for her down-to-earth wisdom and a touch of Midwestern sass, Amanda Beth creates a safe space for transformation that feels both sacred and refreshingly real.

Amanda Beth is the author of *Blooming Into Life: An Energy Healing Journey* and *Stepping Into Power: The Intuitive Path*. Her writing also appears in the *A Daily Gift* series, including A Daily Gift of Kindness, A Daily Gift of Friendship, A Daily Gift of Peace, and A Daily Gift of Inspiration, with more contributions forthcoming. She lives in Iowa, where she continues to explore the meeting place of grounded living and cosmic connection.